Advance Praise

"*Attachment Trauma in Kids* is a must-read book for any foster or adoptive parent struggling to understand and manage their child's behaviors. Debra Wesselmann takes complex neurobiological concepts and translates them into easy-to-understand language that helps empower parents to build trusting relationships with their children. She clearly explains how trauma and neurodivergence impact children's development and how parents can help. I highly recommend this book for clinicians and families alike. It's a game changer!"

—**Jennie Dalcour, MA, LPC,** clinical supervisor and therapist specializing in attachment trauma for Christian Family Care

"As a therapist and an adoptive parent, this book is a much-needed resource. Parenting a child who has faced early trauma can be both exhausting and confusing. Our ability to reflect deeply on our own experiences, our parenting, and what our child is going through can change everything. Debra Wesselmann provides a wealth of knowledge in a relatable way, offering tools and examples that will challenge and empower you and your relationship with your child."

—**Lindsey Ondrak, LIMHP, LPC, IMH-E®,** Nebraska Resource Project for Vulnerable Young Children, University of Nebraska–Lincoln, and owner of Solid Rock Counseling

"This updated edition thoughtfully integrates leading theories on healing attachment trauma in children, offering clear, practical strategies that empower caregivers to support their child's healing. It gently encourages self-reflection, helping caregivers respond to challenging behaviors with greater attunement and trauma-informed insight. It speaks directly to many of the concerns I hear from parents in my work, and I look forward to sharing this wonderful resource with clients."

—**Amanda Walters, LCPC**, postadoption services supervisor at The Baby Fold

"Debra Wesselmann is both validating and hopeful in her approach to explaining the foundations of attachment, attunement, triggers, and other vital concepts. Wesselmann provides specific examples for guidance and tailored reflection, with a psychoeducational experience that is both highly educational and digestible. Whether the reader is a caregiver for children with attachment trauma or a therapist in want of a book to refer to families, this book will be an indispensable asset."

—**Vanessa Summers, LICSW,** therapist and clinical
program manager at Project Harmony, adjunct
instructor at University of Nebraska–Omaha

ATTACHMENT TRAUMA IN KIDS

ATTACHMENT TRAUMA IN KIDS

Integrative Strategies for Parents

Debra Wesselmann

Norton Professional Books

An Imprint of W. W. Norton & Company
Independent Publishers Since 1923

Previous edition published under the title *Integrative Parenting: Strategies for Raising Children Affected by Attachment Trauma.*

Copyright © 2025, 2014 by Debra Wesselmann, Cathy Schweitzer, and Stefanie Armstrong

All rights reserved
Printed in the United States of America

For information about permission to reproduce selections from this book, write to Permissions, W. W. Norton & Company, Inc., 500 Fifth Avenue, New York, NY 10110

For information about special discounts for bulk purchases, please contact W. W. Norton Special Sales at specialsales@wwnorton.com or 800-233-4830

Manufacturing by Versa Press
Production manager: Gwen Cullen

ISBN: 978-1-324-05337-8 (pbk)

W. W. Norton & Company, Inc., 500 Fifth Avenue, New York, NY 10110
www.wwnorton.com

W. W. Norton & Company Ltd., 15 Carlisle Street, London W1D 3BS

1 2 3 4 5 6 7 8 9 0

To my husband, to my kids, and to my grandkids.
You bring me joy every day.

Contents

Acknowledgments

I WANT TO CONVEY MY DEEPEST GRATITUDE to Cathy Schweitzer and Stefanie Armstrong for helping in the creation of the original clinician book and parent guide. They were both instrumental in helping develop the EMDR and family therapy clinical approach and parent strategies. I wish them the best in their work with children and families.

Thank you also to Ann Potter for conceptualizing the three phases of a meltdown and the dominoes approach to behaviors. Her clinical ideas have enhanced my own work for three decades now. Thank you to Erica Liu Wollin for her inspiration, information, and ideas regarding neurodivergence and FASD. I'm indebted to the group of colleagues with whom I work and collaborate on a regular basis for their continued insights, ideas, and encouragement, and my many colleagues in the EMDR community for their inspiration and support. Many thanks to Deborah Malmud and the entire staff at Norton for their guidance in finalizing this work.

And finally, thank you to the parents and children who have let me be a part of their journey. You all were my best teachers over these many years.

Introduction

PARENTS, I'VE UPDATED THIS PARENT GUIDE because you deserve nothing but the best. Raising your traumatized child is an endeavor of the utmost importance, but it can be a task that is confusing, frustrating, and stressful. At times, you may feel hopeless. Whether your child experienced a difficult early environment in your own family or your child was in the care of someone else—and whether your child experienced medical trauma, adverse care, or separations and losses—their development was altered. Methods that worked with other children you raised may not be working with this child. Your emotional well-being may be suffering.

Although my coauthors and I were happy with our first edition of these books, knowledge through new discoveries in the fields of attachment, trauma, and neurobiology has continued to grow, furthering success in our work with parents and traumatized kids. I've also continued to learn from the wonderfully unique families in my clinical practice in the decade since the first books were written and from collaborative efforts with many talented and wise colleagues. It was time to create a second edition clinician manual as well as an updated and revised parent guide with the purpose of offering updated strategies grounded in the latest information about attachment, trauma, and neurobiology. You'll find within this edition methods for overcoming obstacles to building attachment security with your child grounded in the latest science. The information will provide you with a deeper understanding of brain challenges created by developmental traumas as well as by neurodivergence or substance exposure in utero. Equipped with updated knowledge from the fields of attachment and trauma, you'll find new confidence for calming symptoms of dissociation, suicidality, and self-harming, in addition to the many other alarming behaviors exhibited by kids who've endured a traumatic past. This edition invites you to reflect and journal throughout the book's chapters and to address your own emotional overload as well. Keep in mind, there's nothing more meaningful than raising your child and changing the trajectory of their life for the better. It's my wish that my own three decades-long journey of discovery will enhance your own and bring you and your child new hope and connection.

ATTACHMENT
TRAUMA IN KIDS

Chapter 1

Attachment: What's It All About?

IF YOU'RE RAISING A CHILD with a history of attachment trauma, you may be an adoptive or foster parent or guardian of a child who suffered from early loss, neglect, or abuse. You may be a biological parent, but your attachment with your child was impeded by struggles you endured with postpartum depression or substance use—or by your child's early suffering due to medical issues. No matter the reasons for your child's attachment injuries, this book is for you.

If you're a grandparent, aunt, uncle, or other supportive adult, this book is for you as well. The bigger the circle of support for families the better, especially if everyone in the circle is on the same page.

You may be reading this book to learn how to prevent possible problems with your child. Or you're reading this book because your child or teen is already exhibiting behaviors that are bewildering and alarming and nothing you do seems to help. They may be lashing out, arguing, or having meltdowns. They may be harming themselves or feeling suicidal. They may be stealing, lying, hoarding food, or watching pornography. They may be acting out sexually or having toileting problems. They may be refusing to attend school, do schoolwork, or follow directions. They may be struggling to get along with other kids.

You may feel anxious, angry, frustrated, helpless, and confused. You may struggle to get a good night's sleep or find time to yourself. You and your partner may argue about your child. You may try to control your child's behaviors through threats, punishments, and lectures. Even though none of that works, you don't know what else to do. You're not alone. Your difficulties are shared by thousands of other parents raising children or teens with a difficult history.

Following are behaviors that are often seen in affected children and teens. We'll talk more about addressing behaviors in subsequent chapters.

- Clingy and attention seeking with parent
- Arguing
- Defiance/opposition
- Destruction of property
- Quick to anger
- Meltdowns
- Aggression toward people or animals
- Acute jealousy toward siblings
- Stealing
- Hiding food
- Lying
- Running away
- Whining
- Difficulty concentrating
- Hyperactivity
- Excessive masturbation
- Sexualized behaviors toward others
- Self-harming behaviors such as cutting or scratching the skin
- Difficulty falling asleep
- Difficulty staying asleep
- Nightmares
- Minor toileting problems
- Abnormal bathroom behaviors, such as urinating in odd places or smearing feces
- Controlling/bossy toward others
- Does not go to parents for comfort
- Will not accept closeness or comfort
- Withdrawing/shutting down
- Indiscriminate affection with strangers and others

You deserve hope and healing for your child, for yourself, and for your entire family. Let's begin the journey by diving into this phenomenon of attachment.

THE SCIENCE OF ATTACHMENT

You may wonder what the term "attachment" really means. Isn't it the same as love? Actually, attachment is not love. The attachment system drives us to seek closeness and connection with our parents when we're little to help us survive. Without the drive to be connected to our parents, we couldn't live, because we're mammals. All mammals need to stay with their parents for a good while or they'll die.

Attachment isn't love, but it can provide fertile ground from which love can grow, especially if it's the kind of attachment that brings us feelings of security and safety. If the circumstances had been ideal when your child was born, your child would have experienced a safe, secure environment in which all your child's needs for closeness and connection were met. When the parent is sensitive and responsive to their baby's needs, the baby develops trust that their parent cares about them and wants the best for them. Their sense of security allows them to feel comfortable with life and love and closeness and all sorts of emotions—because they know their parent will have their back.

The growing child assumes whatever the parent says or does is meant to be helpful, not hurtful. Their positive assumptions motivate them to follow their directions, listen to their advice, and look up to them as role models.

The Five Building Blocks for Secure Attachment

I conceptualize the following five basic building blocks as critical to secure attachment: (a) emotional attunement and empathic responses; (b) affection; (c) a safe, predictable environment; (d) shared pleasure, play, and fun; and (e) repairs. Kids continue to need these components of secure attachment until they're all grown up. Let's look a little more at each of them.

Building Block 1: Emotional Attunement and Empathic Responses

In ideal circumstances, calm parents think a great deal about the inner experience of their baby or young child. Parents make guesses and explore what may be happening. Could my baby be hungry? Tired? Bored? Anxious? When parents reflect upon their baby's cues with empathy, they naturally respond the best they can to meet their needs. The parents stay aware of their own internal state and manage their emotions so they can take good care of their child. As the child grows they learn to trust and reach out for comfort without shame. They internalize the soothing they receive and eventually learn to soothe themselves. Their healthy relationship with their parent becomes a template for future relationships.

Building Block 2: Affection

When parents have grown up in an affectionate home, they're naturally drawn to physical closeness and demonstrate affection with their baby or young child. There exists plenty of face-to-face contact in optimal situations, and the child gains a sense of self as seen through the loving gaze of their parent. The pleasure of closeness and touch generates the flow of *oxytocin*, the love hormone, in the brains of parents and children, creating a wonderful "falling-in-love" feeling. As the child grows older, they're wired for the good feelings closeness and connection can bring.

Building Block 3: A Safe, Predictable Environment

A safe and predictable home environment helps promote the development of a healthy, calm brain and nervous system. The safe environment has structure, routines, and consistent rules. The expectations are reasonable and in the interest of everyone in the family. The grown-ups in the home protect their children, protect themselves, and protect one another. The safe home allows the child to relax and enjoy closeness with the parent so love can grow. The safe home and safe relationships become the child's secure base from which they can explore the world.

Building Block 4: Shared Pleasure, Play, and Fun

When parents are happy, they're naturally more playful, and they strive to make their baby or young child happy through fun moments together. Oxytocin and other pleasure chemicals are released in the brain, providing even more opportunity for feelings of love to grow. Babies and children learn to engage playfully with siblings and friends, and their nervous system is wired to enjoy their relationships. Relationships continue to be a source of pleasure throughout life.

Building Block 5: Repairs

No parent is perfect. All babies and young children experience moments of misattunement with their parents, because all adults at times become preoccupied or stressed. These moments leave the child feeling hurt or anxious. If parents are reflective and capable of looking at themselves honestly, they're able to recognize when they've caused some hurt or anxiety for their child. By acknowledging their misstep and repairing the breach, they help their child learn those moments aren't the end of the world—that safety and reconnection are always right around the corner. They learn it's safe to express their distress, and that their feelings will be heard and validated.

Positive Memory Networks

As the baby or young child experiences closeness and good feelings with their parent, the good feelings are stored in their brain and they come to believe all kinds of positive things about themselves, others, and the world, such as . . .

- "I can trust that my parent will love me and help me."

- "I can have all kinds of feelings and I'll be okay."
- "I can trust my parent to be in charge and take good care of me."
- "I can ask for help."
- "It's safe to love and trust."
- "I don't have to be perfect."
- "I belong."
- "I'm good, and I deserve good things."
- "The world around me is in general a good place."
- "I can expect good things from others."

Kids with these beliefs naturally turn to their parents for comfort and closeness, and they're also curious to learn more about others. The regions of their brain designed for communicating and connecting with others are well developed. They're eager to explore the world and they're drawn to develop relationships that match the relationships they've had before.

"My Window Is Big"

Figure 1.1 illustrates a wide window of tolerance for distress in the face of hard situations. Early nurturing and attachment security helps kids develop a general sense of safety in the world. With help from their parents, they learn to cope and problem solve, whether they're dealing with math homework, conflict at home or school, or feeling hungry before dinner with an hour to go. The *ventral vagus* nerve is active when they're in this calm state. This nerve is connected to the social and language centers of their brain, allowing them to talk to others about their problems or reach out for comfort (Porges, 2009). Reaching out helps kids stay in ventral vagal functioning and cope even when things get tough.

All of us have such strong emotions at times that we're unable to stay within the window of tolerance. No one goes through life without occasionally getting thrown for a loop. When something is just too much to handle, even with secure attachments in place, the sympathetic nervous system lights up and we move into the *fight-or-flight zone*. We may become aggressive in our tone or body

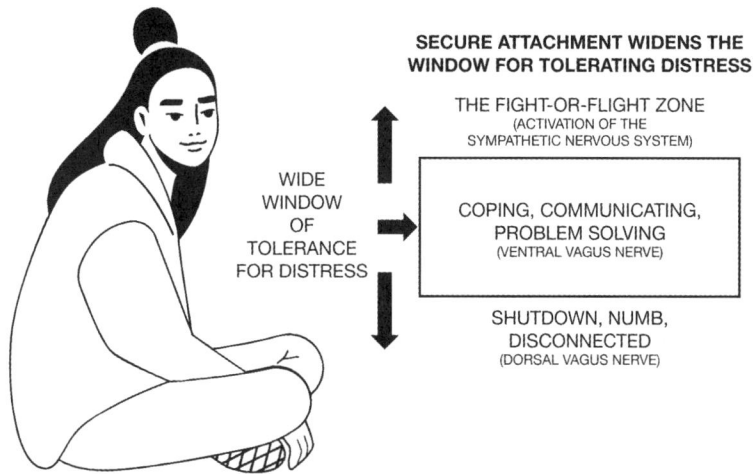

FIGURE 1.1 Secure attachment widens the window of tolerance for distress. *Source: Window of tolerance concept has been described by Ogden et al. (2006), Porges (2009), and Siegel (1999). Illustration by Cathy Solarana.*

posture or we may look and sound fearful or even flee the scene. On the other hand, we may be activated on the inside, but frozen on the outside. If we perceive another person as a threat, our fear may drive us to *fawn*—that is, attempt to pacify the individual in some way to reduce the danger. In the fight-or-flight zone, our system is flooded with cortisol and adrenaline. Our heart and respiration may pick up speed, while our digestive system slows down. We're less able to think, trust, reach out to others, and problem solve. We may spin in uncertainty about what to do.

If the activation is too much for us, we may collapse and shut down. This is a sign that the dorsal ventral part of our nervous system has kicked in. In this shutdown mode, we may even zone out mentally and dissociate from the situation. In the shutdown mode, we can't think properly, problem solve, or let others help.

Even if our window for tolerating distress is usually wide open due to a supportive environment in early life, our window for tolerance can become small temporarily due to circumstances that leave us in a more vulnerable condition. For example, any of us can become more reactive to everyday annoyances on days that we're taxed from exhaustion or illness. It takes extra effort on those days to use our coping skills or use our support system and avoid moving into the fight-or-flight zone.

WHEN CIRCUMSTANCES GET IN THE WAY OF A SECURE ATTACHMENT

Think back to your child's earliest experiences, whether you were their first parent or not. What were the circumstances that got in the way of a secure attachment? Let's consider the building blocks and what can happen in difficult circumstances.

Missing Building Block 1: Emotional Attunement and Empathic Responses

Babies aren't born able to articulate their feelings. It's up to parents to observe and interpret the baby's cues. If you or your child's first parent experienced intense distress and dysregulation or was overwhelmed and shut down, your child didn't experience consistent soothing or reassurance in response to their needs. Or if your child started life with medical needs and interventions that caused pain without relief, there was no opportunity to learn that parents are a source of comfort or that they care. Opportunities for building closeness and connection were missing. There existed a disconnect for the child and perhaps for the parent too.

Missing Building Block 2: Affection

If you or the child's first parents were distressed, shut down, or impaired by substance use, there weren't enough opportunities for physical closeness and pleasure to generate oxytocin and the falling-in-love feeling for both the child and the parent. Or if your child had medical problems, there was no way to experience joy from affectionate touch. In fact, touch may have caused more pain than comfort. Your child likely felt alone and anxious. Their innate needs for closeness and connection remained unmet.

Missing Building Block 3: A Safe, Predictable Environment

If your child experienced their environment as frightening, whether they were in the hospital with bright lights and noises and tubes and needles or in a home where there was fighting or substance abuse and neglect of their needs, their nervous system was in an activated state again and again. They naturally became wired for vigilance and fear. The chronic activation of their nervous system prevented them from learning and reaching developmental milestones as they should.

Missing Building Block 4: Shared Pleasure, Play, and Fun

If you or the child's first parents were overwhelmed, or there were medical needs that got in the way, your child may have missed out on playful interactions that would have provided early experiences of shared joy. They would have missed opportunities to learn how to laugh and feel happy and expect good things from relationships with others. They're at high risk for seeking unhealthy ways to feel pleasure when they're older.

Missing Building Block 5: Repairs

If you or your child's first parents were overwhelmed and missed the cues that signaled there was a breach, there were no repairs when your child was hurt. The hurt and mistrust remained held in your child's nervous system.

Insecure Attachment Patterns in Kids

Nature wires us to protect ourselves one way or another. If children don't feel completely safe and secure within their early environment, they can develop defensive patterns to protect themselves. An early researcher, Mary Ainsworth (1982), first identified various specific attachment patterns observed in children.

If your child felt heard at times but unheard at other times, they may have developed an intense way of expressing their needs in an attempt to make sure they were noticed. They may have learned to be very loud or very dramatic. They take charge of trying to get what they want, and they'll fight for it. Your child may demand attention as their way of getting connection, but even when they get it, they can't trust it or enjoy it. This may be an *ambivalent-resistant attachment pattern*. If your child has this ambivalent-resistant pattern, it may feel to you like nothing you do for your child is enough.

On the other hand, your child or teen may have found they were most successful in getting their needs met if they shut down their needs and feelings. They may have developed strong armor and convinced themselves that they don't need anyone, and this allowed them to cope with the way things were. This may be an *avoidant attachment pattern*. You may feel like your child doesn't want any affection from you. Deep down they want closeness, but they'll never show it, because closeness doesn't feel safe.

Your child or teen may not have landed on just one way of coping. Perhaps neither approach gave your child relief, and so they developed a pattern of vacillating back and forth between intense demands and shutting down. You may feel like a yo-yo as they demand attention from you and then push you away.

Finally, your child may have been left with stored fear associated with attachment trauma. (Read more about attachment trauma in Chapter 2.) When your child's stored trauma is triggered by subconscious reminders, you may see sudden distinct shifts in mood, dramatic meltdowns, or lashing out at others. You may find your nervous system becoming immediately overwhelmed and disorganized in response to your child's nervous system. These observations may indicate that your child has a *disorganized attachment*. This doesn't replace the other patterns. This disorganized pattern in response to triggers exists in addition to the other patterns that you observe.

These self-protective patterns are strong because the human drive to survive is an innate part of us. Reflecting upon our child's patterns and triggers can help us attune to the anxiety underlying their behaviors.

What attachment pattern clues do you observe in your child or teen?

☐ 1. My child is loud and vocal about what they want.
☐ 2. My child seeks connection by looking for attention.
☐ 3. My child misbehaves when I'm paying attention to another child in the family.
☐ 4. My child pushes me away.
☐ 5. My child acts as if they don't need me or anyone.
☐ 6. My child doesn't show vulnerable emotions.
☐ 7. My child's mood will switch on a dime.
☐ 8. I never know what will set my child off.
☐ 9. I feel overwhelmed and disorganized in my own nervous system when my child becomes dysregulated.

Numbers 1, 2, and 3 may indicate an ambivalent-resistant attachment pattern.

Numbers 4, 5, and 6 may indicate an avoidant attachment pattern.

Numbers 7, 8, and 9 may indicate a disorganized attachment pattern.

"My Window Is Small"

In another life, your child's nervous system would have been nurtured to a healthy, regulated state through blissful experiences of connection and safety. Their prefrontal brain would have developed a plethora of well-developed connections for thinking, problem solving, and managing emotions and healthy structures in their lower brain for responding appropriately to cues in the environment.

If your child or teen missed out on the early soothing that would have nurtured a healthy nervous system, and they lack a sense of safety in the world that early secure attachment would have provided, their nervous system was left to function in a more primitive way. Furthermore, feelings of mistrust, danger, insecurity, lack of belonging, shame, and worthlessness stored in their memory networks create ongoing underlying anxiety while their attachment fears keep them from seeking and finding comfort. In addition, trauma has impacted brain development and interrupted social and emotional development (more about that in Chapter 2).

Because tolerance is small, your child or teen quickly moves into the fight-or-flight zone where they're unable to cope or think effectively and their behaviors are dysregulated. If that becomes more than their nervous system can handle, they move into the shutdown zone, collapsed and numb. Figure 1.2 illustrates the narrow window of tolerance for distress in which ventral vagal functioning is easily lost.

Your child or teen exhibits their most concerning behaviors when they're outside their window of tolerance for distress. Unfortunately, their mistrust and perceptions of danger keep them on the edge of their window so that even the slightest trigger can catapult them into the fight-or-flight zone.

Over time, you can help your child by attuning to their emotions and providing sensitive, affectionate responses when

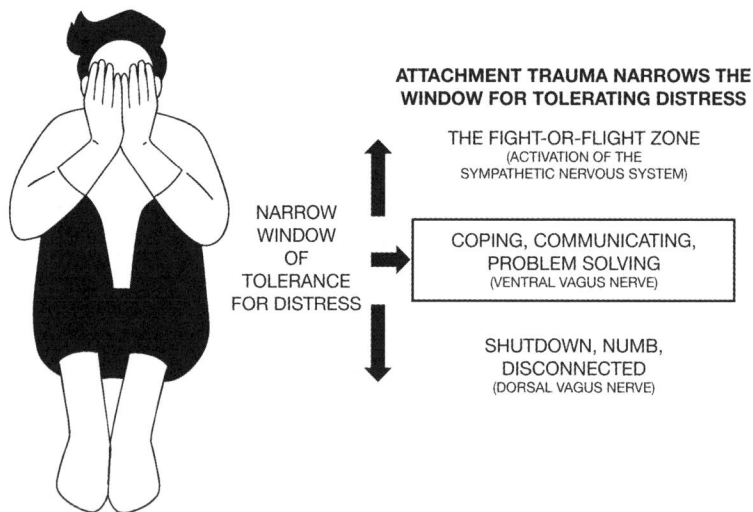

ATTACHMENT TRAUMA NARROWS THE WINDOW FOR TOLERATING DISTRESS

THE FIGHT-OR-FLIGHT ZONE
(ACTIVATION OF THE SYMPATHETIC NERVOUS SYSTEM)

NARROW WINDOW OF TOLERANCE FOR DISTRESS

COPING, COMMUNICATING, PROBLEM SOLVING
(VENTRAL VAGUS NERVE)

SHUTDOWN, NUMB, DISCONNECTED
(DORSAL VAGUS NERVE)

FIGURE 1.2 Attachment trauma narrows the window of tolerance for distress. *Source: The window of tolerance concept has been described by Ogden et al. (2006), Porges (2009), and Siegel (1999). Illustration by Cathy Solorana.*

they're at the edge of their window, half in and half out. This is when they may be most receptive to some *co-regulation*. Co-regulation involves connection and comfort from you to calm their nervous system. (You'll read more about co-regulation in Chapter 5.)

Putting on Your Detective's Hat

With intention, you can strengthen your capacity to attune to your child's nervous system and your own. This is empowering, as calming ourselves or our child is much easier when we're able to recognize the clues to dysregulation early on. Consider the Window of Tolerance figures (1.1 and 1.2) and reflect upon what you've observed in your child and yourself up until now as you answer the following:

How can you tell when your child or teen is operating from within their window of tolerance?

_____

_____

_____

How can you tell when your child or teen is hovering between the ventral vagal calm state and the fight-or-flight zone?

_____

_____

_____

How can you tell if your child or teen is moving into the dorsal vagal shutdown zone?

_____

_____

_____

What have you noticed helps calm your child's nervous system when they're starting to move toward the fight-or-flight zone or shutting down?

_____

_____

_____

How can you tell when you're starting to move toward the fight-or-flight zone?

_____

_____

_____

What do you notice when you're moving into the shutdown zone?

_____

_____

_____

What strategies have helped you calm your nervous system in the past?

_____

_____

_____

Chapter 2

The Trouble With Trauma

TRAUMA IS INDEED TROUBLE. Normal events are processed and integrated in the brain in a way that's helpful to each of us daily. Information we need is stored where it should be stored and information that we don't need is discarded.

However, when something extremely upsetting happens, the processing system in our brain gets overloaded. It shuts down, and the memory gets stored in our brain in a raw form so that the old feelings are easily triggered by any present-day reminder (Shapiro, 2018, p. 37). When this happens, we may not have any idea that past memories are the cause. When your child is triggered, they're likely flooded with upset feelings and no awareness as to why. They also may be prone to nightmares, depression, anxiety, and other mental health symptoms.

Furthermore, kids develop lots of negative beliefs about themselves, others, and the world from early trauma. For example, they may learn "I'm bad, I'm defective, I'll never measure up." They may learn "I'm not safe, others are mean, I have to protect myself, it's not safe to trust." They may learn "The world is dangerous, I'm not safe anywhere, I don't belong."

Besides learning to view themselves and the world through a negative lens, kids impacted by trauma typically fall behind in certain areas developmentally. When their mental energy is focused on coping with stress and staying vigilant, there is little left over for acquiring skills and new information.

Trauma also interferes with the development of trust. It doesn't

feel safe to depend upon their parents to meet their needs or protect them. And there's a specific aspect of trust, called *epistemic
trust*, that is damaged. Epistemic trust means "I trust you and
therefore I trust what you teach me." Lack of epistemic trust leads
kids to mistrust what their parents say or attempt to teach them.
They become suspicious of things others tell them as well. Lack of
epistemic trust interferes with learning from parents and others.
Kids who lack epistemic trust make negative assumptions about
the motivations of others: "Are they lying?" "Are they out to get
me?" "Are they trying to trick me or hurt me?"

WHAT EXACTLY IS ATTACHMENT TRAUMA?

Attachment trauma is any disturbing event or series of events that
cause a child to feel anxious, fearful, or vigilant when they're with
one or both attachment figures.

Neglect

For kids in situations that involve neglect, often due to parents'
stressful circumstances, mental illness, substance use, or due to
orphanage care, the feeling of insignificance and lack of nurturing or protection is traumatic. One young boy I worked with had
been removed from his biological home due to neglect and parental substance addiction. He had meltdowns in his adoptive home
when his family members were occupied and not paying attention to him. I asked him what he felt when people weren't paying attention to him. I asked, "Does it make you feel unseen?"
He wasn't sure. I tried again. "Does it make you feel unheard?"
He still wasn't sure. Then I asked, "Does it make you feel like you
don't exist?" He screamed, "That's it! I don't exist!" My heart went
out to him. I couldn't imagine what it would feel like to question
your very existence.

On top of that, kids who had experienced early neglect often
describe memories of being hungry and wet with no one to feed
them or change them. They describe being alone in the dark with

no one to comfort them. If they were too young to retain conscious memories, it doesn't matter. The fearful feelings are carried on into their present life.

Verbal Abuse, Physical Abuse, or Sexual Abuse

Any of the above types of maltreatment constitute attachment trauma if a parent perpetrated the abuse. The child is left in a double bind. The person to whom they wish to run for help is the source of the emotional and/or physical injury.

Sometimes the parent is not overtly mistreating the child but is failing to protect the child from another family member or someone else. In other cases, the parent has no idea that the child is being mistreated by someone, but the child still feels unprotected. Either way, the trauma leads to mistrust and anxiety related to the nonoffending parent.

Early Medical Trauma

Infants and young children in pain or separated due to medical problems and interventions don't understand. The adults are likely doing everything they can to help the child, but the youngster ends up believing the world isn't safe and there's no one upon whom they can depend to make the pain go away or fix their fear. This is a heartbreaking situation for parents and children.

Being in the Care of a Parent Suffering From Mental Illness or Addiction

Infants and young children are wired to watch the parent's face for reassurance regarding their safety. When a parent's face, voice, or behaviors are confusing and frightening, the child wants to go to the parent for comfort, but the parent is also the source of their fear. In a home affected by mental illness or addiction, the environment is unpredictable and unsafe. Even if the child's environment becomes temporarily calm, their nervous system remains on high alert.

Loss of a Parent

When children suffer loss of a parent to whom they had an attachment, their grief doesn't easily subside. They're wired to seek closeness and connection with the parent who's missing from their life. The loss may be due to a planned adoption as a newborn or a placement in foster care following neglect or abuse in the biological home. The loss may be due to the disappearance of one of the parents after a divorce. The loss may be due to the death of a parent.

In the aftermath, the child is likely mistrusting and afraid to love or get close to another parent. The feelings of grief and loss may be triggered by closeness to anyone else. They may be troubled by nightmares, depression, and anxiety.

The term "ambiguous loss" describes a loss for which there is no finality or resolution (Boss, 2000). This is true for many children and teens in foster or adoptive care. The parent is gone from their life, yet they know the parent is *somewhere*. The child or teen is unable to know where they are, what they're doing, who they're with, or if they have other children or significant relationships. They don't know whether the parent still thinks of them or feels badly for what happened, whether they loved them, and if they're okay. They're often confused and struggling to figure it all out, even though there's no way to do that. They may be imagining all kinds of scenarios about their parent, and they're left with a sense of confusion over who they are. This kind of ambiguity complicates their grief.

The Attachment That Never Was

Another type of attachment trauma involves the absence of anyone to whom the child can attach from the time of birth or soon after. If your child was placed immediately into orphanage care or moved from home to home in foster care before your child came to join you, there may have been no opportunity for learning how to attach or how to trust any caregiver. Infants are driven to attach to someone for survival purposes. If no one has ever been there, it's life-threatening and deeply traumatizing. Often, the only way to cope is to completely shut down the needs and desires for closeness. It becomes all about self-protection and operating in survival mode, taking care of their own needs however they can. Knowing right from wrong is completely irrelevant when there's no one but you to keep yourself safe and alive. Once a child begins operating in this mode, it's hard to learn to believe that any adult could be trusted to care for them.

Social and Cultural Trauma

Many kids with a history of trauma and loss have experiences of rejection, marginalization, or discrimination based on being a part of a group that is different from their present family or from the majority of their neighbors or peers. The differences may be related to ethnicity, culture, religion, gender identity, romantic preference, or physical differences due to disabilities. The feeling of being different from others can lead to a sense of being in the "out group," which is difficult in and of itself. And the reality is that these differences can lead to experiences of being rejected, demeaned, or treated as invisible by certain other peers or adults. It's easy for us as parents to be unaware of either overt or covert experiences of rejection our child may be experiencing in the community or at school or even from extended family members.

Trauma in the Earliest Years—Does It Really Matter?

Even if all of your child's trauma happened prior to age 2 and they have no recall of what happened, the *feelings* associated with the events are still stored and may be activated with subconscious reminders. Whether the preverbal trauma involves painful medical interventions or early foster or orphanage care, the fear and hurt present at the time may be stuck in the emotional parts of the brain, causing the child or teen to push people away or experience anxiety and depression in the present day.

Luckily, it's not necessary for children to remember early events to find healing. Armed with evidence-based trauma treatment methods, therapists can help kids even if they cannot recall or describe the traumatic events. Furthermore, by using the integrative parenting strategies, parents can increase the security of the attachment relationship and calm their child's nervous system over time.

Check the events that happened to your child:

☐ Loss of, and/or changes in, primary caregivers

☐ Temporary placement, such as foster care or orphanage care

☐ Physical abuse

☐ Sexual abuse

☐ Rejection or verbal abuse

☐ Physical neglect

☐ Emotional neglect

☐ Early frightening or painful medical interventions

☐ Early experiences of pain that may have interfered with the child's ability to relax and bond, such as ear pain or colic

☐ Early separations from primary caregivers due to hospitalizations or any other reasons

☐ Frequent changes in day care providers

☐ A frightening or chaotic environment, such as domestic violence, which may have interfered with the child's ability to relax and bond

☐ Parental addictions that may have removed the safe emotional presence of the parent

☐ Parental stressors, such as illness in the family, death in the family, job loss, and so on, that may have removed the safe emotional presence of the parent

☐ Parental emotional problems, such as posttraumatic stress disorder (PTSD), that may have removed the safe emotional presence of the parent

☐ The child's overhearing of information that interfered with feelings of safety and trust in parents

☐ Ridicule or rejection from classmates or teachers

☐ Discrimination or marginalization experiences in the community, the school, or the family

☐ Other: _____

_____

Trauma and Development

Imagine you're hiking along a beautiful path in the woods, and you're looking forward to what you might see. Unfortunately, your hike is interrupted when you fall and sprain your ankle, then hide from a family of grizzly bears, put salve on a bee sting, and later take cover from a sudden rainstorm. Your whole focus becomes just surviving this miserable journey somehow, and by the time you reach the end, you have no memories for the birds or the flowers or the trees.

Growing up is supposed to provide lots of opportunities for making friends, playing, talking, listening, and learning to solve problems, tolerate frustration, make good decisions, and much more. If the journey of growing up is more about just surviving each day, there may be very little opportunity for the childhood experiences needed to develop socially, emotionally, and cognitively.

Trauma and the Brain

Researchers now have the opportunity to investigate the impact of early trauma on the development of the brain through various types of scans. What they've discovered is that early chronic abuse or neglect has a direct impact on the development and functioning of many regions of the brain. For example, Martin Teicher and his colleagues (2016) found that the corpus callosum, the region responsible for right-brain and left-brain communication, does not develop properly in children who have been traumatized. This leaves them with poor right-brain–left-brain communication and poor left-brain capacity to manage right-brain emotions.

The prefrontal brain, sometimes called the upstairs brain because it's just behind the forehead, is typically underdeveloped in kids who experienced early chronic abuse or neglect. The underdeveloped prefrontal brain leaves the child with impaired executive functions. They typically have poor focus, poor impulse control, and poor problem-solving ability. The "downstairs" emotional regions of the brain also develop differently for kids living in an unsafe environment. They're left easily triggered to experience intense reactions of anxiety, fear, or anger.

All of these brain effects are nature's way of keeping kids ready to run or fight or freeze to survive a dangerous environment. Unfortunately, although these responses may have been helpful back in primitive times, they're not helpful for children or their families in today's world. They struggle to cope, to control their emotions, to focus and learn, or develop trust and closeness in their present relationships.

The Complication of Further Brain-Based Problems

Many kids affected by attachment trauma were also exposed to alcohol or drugs in utero. Parent substance addiction is, after all, a common factor in early neglect and abuse. Chapter 6 describes the many effects of substance exposure on the structure and functioning of the brain.

It's also not uncommon for kids affected by attachment trauma to have conditions related to neurodivergence, which simply means there are differences in the structure and functioning of their brain at birth. There exists a wide spectrum from mild to more extreme neurodivergence and there are a variety of possible brain differences, from challenges related to functioning somewhere on the autism spectrum to the challenges of attention-deficit/hyperactivity disorder (ADHD) or learning disabilities.

Children affected by in utero substance exposure, kids who are neurodivergent, and kids with a history of attachment trauma are all at high risk for sensory processing disorder due to their brain differences. Sensory problems can cause children to experience input from their senses more strongly than typical kids or have less capacity to notice the input. Sometimes they swing from one extreme to the other. The atypical way in which their brain processes sensory input easily activates and dysregulates their nervous system.

More information on parenting strategies for supporting kids with brain-based challenges is provided in Chapter 6.

Mixed-Up Thinking

Experiences that were sad or frightening for your child remain stored in a raw form along with the associated feelings and beliefs. Their beliefs may have actually been true at one point, even though they're no longer true. However, just as someone who unknowingly wears sunglasses indoors believes the room to be dark, a child whose perceptions are shaped by past trauma sees the world through that lens with unwavering certainty. As you complete the checklist that follows, think about how your child's negative beliefs impact their present-day perceptions, emotions, and actions.

Consider your child's past traumas and present behaviors and make some educated guesses about the negative beliefs that may trouble your child:

☐ "There's no one to help me."
☐ "It's not safe to trust my parents to care about what I need."
☐ "I'm not important."
☐ "I can't get what I need."
☐ "I'm not safe."
☐ "I can't get the closeness and love I need."
☐ "It's not safe to have needs or feelings."
☐ "I'm not good enough."
☐ "I'm a mistake."
☐ "It's not safe to love."
☐ "I'm all alone."
☐ "There's no one to whom I can go for comfort."
☐ "Bad things will happen."
☐ "I will always be rejected and abandoned."
☐ "Parents are mean."
☐ "Parents leave."
☐ "I don't belong anywhere."
☐ "It's not safe to trust or get close."
☐ Other: _____

_____

Because of the drive to survive, children subconsciously make rules to protect themselves when their environment is unsafe. Their rules become part of them, and they stick with them, even when their environment changes for the better. As you complete the following checklist, remember that fear drives your child to follow these rules.

Consider your child's past and the behaviors you see today and make some educated guesses about your child's survival rules:

- ☐ "I must take care of getting my own needs met by myself, in any way I can."
- ☐ "I must take what I need/want whenever I have the chance."
- ☐ "I must cry and demand so that you'll hear me and attend to me."
- ☐ "I must not trust or depend on anyone."
- ☐ "I must put up walls to protect myself."
- ☐ "I must be vigilant to danger and mistrust others at all times."
- ☐ "I must stay in control of my environment to stay safe."
- ☐ "I must fight to defend myself at all costs."
- ☐ "I must be ready to run to survive."
- ☐ "I must not share my thoughts or feelings."
- ☐ "I must blend into the woodwork. I must hide myself."

For your child, making changes to these rules feels dangerous.

Triggers, Triggers, Everywhere

If your child or teen experienced attachment trauma early in life (even if they don't remember it), their nervous system became wired for self-protection, leading to heightened vigilance and mistrust. Common, everyday situations or parenting behaviors can fire up their nervous system in an instant and lead to challenging behaviors. The lists that follow will help you gain greater awareness and insight regarding your child's triggers.

Check the nurturing behaviors that seem to trigger your child:

- □ Being hugged or held
- □ Affectionate words
- □ Being tucked into bed
- □ Being cared for when sick
- □ Praise

If you checked the above triggers, your child's earliest experience most likely led them to believe they were bad and that adults aren't trustworthy. Therefore, they're unable to trust the intentions behind your kind words or behaviors. Instead of activating the pleasure circuits, the experience of being cared for activates stored trauma. The integrative parenting strategies described throughout this book will help your child learn to trust and receive love over time.

Check any of these situations that seem to trigger your child:

- □ Being sent to bed
- □ Noticing you talking with someone else on the phone or in person
- □ Observing you caring for a sibling
- □ Being around you when you're busy or distracted

All kids need connection, and it's normal for kids to let us know with their behaviors when they're feeling shut out. But if your child exhibits intense reactions to these situations on a regular basis, their early needs were likely unmet. Circumstances left them feeling unseen, unheard, and alone. Instead of viewing your child's behaviors as attention-seeking, try to understand them as connection-seeking. The integrative parenting strategies will help build your child's trust and connection with you over time.

Check any of these situations that are triggers for your child:

- □ Corrections or redirections by an adult
- □ Questions (such as "Did you do that?" or "Why did you do that?")

□ Saying "no"
□ An adult's angry, sad, or frustrated face
□ An adult's stern tone

While most kids resist correction at times, frequent, intense reactions are likely related to a deep reserve of painful memories and a shortage of positive experiences. Your child's early experiences shaped the belief that they are inherently flawed and that parents or other adults couldn't genuinely care for them, leading them to assume negative intentions.

Check any of these situations that trigger your child:

□ The sight of something enticing
□ Being told they have to wait for a desired thing, food, or activity
□ Approaching a birthday or Christmas
□ Other triggering situations involving waiting: _____

_____

_____

Of course, all kids struggle with waiting for good things. But if your child becomes consistently overwhelmed by waiting or anticipating something good, they likely learned early on that good things don't come to them and that they can't trust adults to keep their promises. Furthermore, the area of the prefrontal brain that assists us with tolerating frustration is negatively impacted by developmental trauma and also by autism, ADHD, prenatal alcohol exposure or other substance exposure.

Naturally, your child struggles to find ways to soothe their anxiety. Many kids with a history of attachment trauma seek relief through methods that provide immediate but short-term gratification. Examples including consuming comfort foods, sexualized activities, taking things that don't belong to them, or obsessive use of video games. Teens and older children are at risk for compulsive use of pornography, alcohol, or other substances to fix their feelings.

Write down ways in which your child or teen tries to find comfort for themselves:

_____

_____

_____

_____

What Is My Child's Diagnosis, Anyway?

Children and teens with a history of attachment trauma may have any of a number of diagnoses, and they can be difficult to diagnose due to their complexity. Only qualified mental health clinicians can provide diagnoses after a thorough evaluation of your child. Sometimes specialized psychological or neuropsychological testing is required to properly diagnose kids with difficult histories and behaviors.

Your child or teen may meet criteria for one or more diagnoses related to their behaviors. One common diagnosis for kids with an attachment trauma history is oppositional defiant disorder, indicated by an ongoing pattern of defiance, arguing, and angry behaviors. Another common diagnosis, intermittent explosive disorder, is indicated by frequent explosions, at least two per week, that don't cause actual damage, or physical explosions every few months that do cause injury or damage. Teens with a history of attachment trauma are also at high risk for substance use disorders.

Your child or teen may have diagnoses related to depressed mood or intense anxiety. In addition to mental health problems that stem from their early traumas, your child may have mental health problems that are part of their genetic makeup. Symptoms of an inherent mental illness are worsened by trauma.

Your child or teen may meet criteria for a formal diagnosis of PTSD related to the traumas they've endured. Criteria include some form of intrusive memories, nightmares, or intense reactivity to reminders of traumatic events along with negative beliefs and moods and avoidance of reminders of the past. Traumatic

stress symptoms may be accompanied by symptoms of dissociation in which they lose connection to where they are and what's
happening right now.

You may have heard the term "reactive attachment disorder"
(RAD), or this diagnosis may have been given to your child. Not
all kids with attachment trauma and disturbed attachment patterns have a diagnosis of RAD. This diagnosis is a trauma-related
diagnosis that is usually reserved for kids who have had little
chance to form an attachment with anyone due to severe early
neglect, frequent changes in caregivers, or orphanage care. They
have episodes of sadness, irritability, or fearfulness but only rarely
seek comfort and also don't appear to respond to comfort for the
most part.

Disinhibited social engagement disorder is a trauma-related
diagnosis reserved for children with the same history of neglect,
repeated changes in caregivers, or orphanage care who will seek
affection from any adult and go off with strangers without hesita-
tion. They don't check back with their present parents and they're
not afraid of leaving them.

Your child may also exhibit characteristics of fetal alcohol spectrum disorder (FASD), autism spectrum disorder (ASD), and
ADHD. These diagnoses are sometimes difficult to recognize and
the symptoms can be difficult to differentiate from symptoms
related to attachment trauma. (Read more about these conditions
in Chapter 6.)

There are many other possible diagnoses that may be related
to a difficult early life and possible inherited mental health conditions as well. Psychiatrist and researcher Bessel van der Kolk
(2005) proposed a new diagnosis—developmental trauma
disorder—for acceptance into the fifth edition of the *Diagnostic and
Statistical Manual of Mental Disorders* (American Psychiatric Association, 2013). The diagnosis was not approved but if it were to
get approval, it could replace other commonly used diagnoses for
many children and teens with a history of attachment trauma.
Criteria would include the array of symptoms we observe that

currently result in multiple diagnoses while highlighting developmental trauma and its effect on attachment, emotion regulation, and social and emotional development as the direct cause for the symptoms of mood, interpersonal problems, and difficult behaviors. Although the proposed diagnosis was not entered into the current diagnostic manual, efforts continue for inclusion in a future manual.

Talk to your child's mental health care providers if you have questions concerning their diagnoses or the need for an evaluation.

Attachment Trauma Therapy for Children and Teens

There are two evidence-based approaches for treating kids with trauma that have received a number 1 rating from the California Evidence-Based Clearinghouse for Child Welfare (2010). The organization is a highly respected nonprofit that researches and distributes information regarding the best methods for helping kids. One evidence-based approach is trauma-focused cognitive-behavioral therapy, which teaches emotional coping skills and uses a narrative approach to help kids overcome their trauma. The other evidence-based approach with a number 1 rating for treating trauma is *eye movement desensitization and reprocessing* (EMDR). EMDR for children is also endorsed by other organizations around the world including the World Health Organization (2013) and the United Kingdom's National Institute for Health and Care Excellence (2018).

EMDR improves symptoms for kids and adults affected by any type of trauma. If your child or teen is involved in EMDR therapy, the therapist may ask your child to follow the therapist's fingers or a puppet or wand from side to side, or follow lights on a horizontal light bar. Alternatively, the EMDR therapist may tap back and forth on your child's knees or hands, or place small buzzers, called *tactile pulsars*, in your child's hands. The stimulation lights up centers in your child's right and left hemispheres vital for assistance with processing emotions and reducing a variety of symptoms and behaviors related to many types of traumas.

The accompanying clinician manual for this book, *EMDR and Family Therapy: Integrative Treatment for Attachment Trauma in Children* (Wesselmann, 2025), offers an approach that combines EMDR with family therapy to treat the array of symptoms and problems caused by attachment trauma. Early research on the integrative method shows promising results (Dreckmeier-Meiring, 2024; Swimm, 2018; van der Hoeven et al., 2023; Wesselmann et al., 2018).

The integrative approach begins with psychoeducation and specialized EMDR and family therapy activities designed to improve trust and connection, emotion regulation, communication, and problem-solving in your home. Later, a therapeutic story is created followed by EMDR through gentle methods that help heal your child's traumas and triggers. Your emotional support is critical to helping your child face their difficult past and feel what they need to feel to heal.

There are numerous studies of EMDR successfully treating a very wide variety of symptoms and disorders. A list of studies can be found at the EMDR Institute of Francine Shapiro, the founder of EMDR (EMDR.com).

Is Medication Bad for Kids?

Kids and adults suffering from mood, attentional, and behavioral problems often require medication assistance. The impact of early trauma on brain development as well as heredity can lead to problematic brain chemistry. We can't change our brain chemistry for the better with sheer willpower. Brain chemistry can be a barrier to rational thinking, problem solving, and finding new perspectives. At the same time, kids with a history of attachment trauma are complicated. Medication providers have to consider the child's traumatic history as well as possible inherited conditions, substance abuse exposure, or neurodivergence. Furthermore, kids' brains are still developing and their hormones are changing. Finding a medication provider with the appropriate expertise to assess your child regarding the possibility of treatment with medication is critical.

Chapter 3

The Nuts and Bolts of Mentalization

THE TERM "MENTALIZATION" is not a term used in everyday speech, so don't feel badly if you've never heard of it before. The term makes me think of *mentalists*, those performers who claim to read minds and manipulate others' thoughts with special powers. I wish we could all develop special powers to read our kids' thoughts and change them. Mentalization can't do that but it is still a powerful tool. Mentalization will help you carry out every single strategy in this book with far more effectiveness.

THE POWER OF MENTALIZATION

Researchers Peter Fonagy and his colleagues (1997) were the first to discover that parents who are skillful with mentalizing can more easily form secure attachments with their kids. He explains that mentalizing is the ability to pay attention to what's going on inside of ourselves and inside of others. This skill helps us create a wonderful connection with our kids, because it helps us with the most important building block for secure attachment–emotional attunement and empathic responses. Mentalization helps us stay alert to our child's cues and also stay on top of our own internal state so that negative feelings or thoughts don't get in our way.

Mentalizing State = Making No Assumptions

When we're in a mentalizing state, we're curious and open-minded without making assumptions about anything. Confidence may be a good thing when it comes to performing as a mentalist, but when it comes to mentalizing regarding the internal state of our kids, too much confidence is a bad thing. If we think we know everything about our kids, it's a sign that we're not good mentalizers. If we think we don't know enough and we want to learn more, we're more likely to listen and attune to their emotions.

Mentalizing State = Letting Go of Judgments

Another important aspect of mentalization is the ability to let go of judgments. Judgments stop us from learning and understanding. When we stay nonjudgmental, we listen better. We try to understand our kids more deeply. We reflect on our child's history and all the factors contributing to their actions, and so we respond with greater sensitivity.

Mentalizing State = Attuning to Our Own Internal State

In a mentalizing state, we pay attention to our own thoughts, emotions, and behaviors. We're more self-aware in a mentalizing state and able to check ourselves if we get overwhelmed by negative emotions or thoughts.

Mentalizing State = Reflecting on Our Missteps

In a mentalizing state, we're able to reflect on the consequences of our actions or words. When we recognize we've said or done something that's hurt our child's feelings, we can own our misstep and make a repair.

Being Human

No one can be in a mentalizing state 100% of the time. We're all vulnerable to judgments and assumptions and reactivity when we're stressed or our mood is low. When our nervous system starts ramping up and our survival brain lights up, we become more vigilant, which can really get in our way.

Staying in your calm window and a mentalizing state can be especially challenging if you carry trauma within your own nervous system. However, with conscious intention, you can develop tools to help you expand your window of tolerance and increase your capacity to stay in a mentalizing state. Having your own therapist can also make all the difference in your ability to expand your window of tolerance for all areas of your life.

The Pause

Training ourselves to take a pause as soon as we notice ourselves getting activated can help us get back on track when we lose the mentalizing state. Stepping back and taking a couple of deep breaths or taking a quick walk can interrupt the activation. Self-talk for self-calming is a skill everyone needs. If you find yourself activated by your child's behaviors, remind yourself, "My child's behavior is driven by trauma and an overactive nervous system." Reflect upon the traumas that led your child to become vigilant, reactive, and mistrusting. The pause gives you a chance for some self-talk.

Developing habits that help you calm your own nervous system will make it easier for you to take the pause and use your tools. Many parents find it helpful to download mindfulness and meditation apps on their phone to use on a regular basis. Many find it helpful to find a yoga class or get regular massages. One parent I know bought a massage chair to use each night. Many parents also benefit from finding or developing local support groups with other parents. Definitely consider finding a therapist to help.

NEGATIVE THOUGHTS: EVERYBODY HAS THEM

The stress caused by a child's difficult behaviors can trigger automatic negative thoughts for most parents. If you find it difficult to access an accepting, open, mentalizing demeanor when you're struggling with your child, you are not alone. These thoughts are automatic and come from a very primitive place. You're most likely to be vulnerable to negative thoughts when your nervous system is becoming activated and you're moving outside of your window of tolerance. Identifying the thoughts that are most common for you will help you grab ahold of them early, take a pause, breathe, and initiate some helpful self-talk to bring yourself back into your calm window.

Check any negative thoughts you sometimes have when you're triggered:

☐ "My child hates me."
☐ "My child is a bad kid."
☐ "My child is just spoiled."
☐ "My child deserves punishment."
☐ "This is hopeless. I give up."
☐ "I'm a bad parent."
☐ "I can't do this anymore."
☐ "I need to show my child who's the boss."
☐ Other: _____

_____

Think back on challenging situations with your child and identify your automatic emotions:

☐ Anger
☐ Frustration
☐ Hurt
☐ Guilt
☐ Shame
☐ Embarrassment
☐ Fear
☐ Anxiety

Check the self-talk reminders you think will be most helpful. Write them down so you can grab them when you need them or type them into your phone:

☐ "My child has an overactive nervous system caused by past trauma."
☐ "My child doesn't have the capacity to control this right now."
☐ "My child wants to be close but feels scared of rejection."
☐ "My child is terrified of being vulnerable."

- ☐ "My child needs to feel in control in order to feel safe."
- ☐ "My child is trying to fill an emotional void."
- ☐ "My child is trying to self-soothe."
- ☐ "Wants feel like needs to my child."
- ☐ "Trauma changed my child's brain."
- ☐ "My child's behaviors are driven by the primitive survival brain."
- ☐ "My child is desperate to feel better."
- ☐ "When my child's nervous system is on fire, the thinking brain is offline."
- ☐ "My child lives in self-protective mode with no way out."
- ☐ "I can pause, breathe, and respond effectively."
- ☐ "With intention, I can use the integrative strategies."
- ☐ "Over time, I can make a difference in my child's life."
- ☐ "Over time, I can strengthen safe connection and help calm my child's nervous system."

Journaling on a regular basis can increase your capacity to mentalize and reflect. You might begin each day by journaling answers to some of the following questions:

- What is my goal as a parent today? _____
  _____
  _____

- What thoughts or feelings might get in my way? _____
  _____
  _____

- What might help me stay calm and reflective today? _____
  _____
  _____

Chapter 4

Building Connection Against the Odds

MOVING YOUR CHILD OR TEEN toward greater attachment security is clearly key to bringing forward the person they're meant to be, developing trust, and creating a more genuine connection. That said, how do you provide the building blocks for attachment security with kids who put up roadblocks and obstacles to closeness at every turn?

HOW CAN I ATTUNE AND EMPATHIZE WHEN MY CHILD'S EMOTIONS DON'T MAKE ANY SENSE?

Building Block 1 involves emotional attunement and empathic responses. For the child or teen who's vigilant and mistrusting, the smallest thing can send their nervous system into fight or flight. They live life on the edge of their window of tolerance so that something that's a little deal becomes a big deal in a nanosecond. Their nervous system keeps them ready to self-protect at all times. Our natural response to kids' over-the-top reactions is to say, "Knock off the drama and settle down!" That's what makes attunement and empathy so difficult!

However, an attuned connection with you can help their nervous system find a sense of safety. So even if their feelings and thoughts are completely irrational, attunement and empathy can bring safety and greater calm. The key here is that you can attune and empathize with their emotions without validating their perceptions. Once they feel a sense of connection, it is possible to provide a more reasonable perspective.

In the following vignette, Joseph's dad responds to his avoidant pattern with attunement:

Joseph is a teenager with avoidant attachment tendencies. He came home from school late, went into his bedroom, and slammed the door.

> **Dad:** (*Thinks "To heck with him. If he's going to be rude and sit in his room, it's not my problem." But he takes a pause and steps into a mentalizing state. He remembers Joseph's stored memories of rejection and feels compassion for his struggles. He knocks on Joseph's door.*) Joseph, can I come in for a minute?
>
> **Joseph:** Yeah, what do you want?
>
> **Dad:** (*Sitting down on the bed*) I'm just a little concerned. Can you help me understand what's going on?
>
> **Joseph:** I had a late paper and had a detention. I had to take the stupid late bus.
>
> **Dad:** Sounds like you had a hard day. I love you, son.
>
> **Joseph:** Hmm.
>
> **Dad:** I had detentions sometimes, too, as a kid. It certainly wasn't my favorite thing. (*Joseph's dad felt no need to talk about the late paper. Joseph had already faced the consequences.*) Tonight will be better. We're having spaghetti in about an hour. Sound good?
>
> **Joseph:** Yeah, I guess.

In the following vignette, Kaishawn's mom prioritizes connection over correction:

> **Mom:** Hi, Kaishawn, how was your day?
>
> **Kaishawn [age 12]:** (*Slams the door*) Crappy! I hate school. Mr. Smith is a jerk!
>
> **Mom:** (*Holds herself back from correcting his language or his door slamming*) It sounds like you had a rough day. Do you want to talk about it?
>
> **Kaishawn:** I turned in the wrong math page for homework. Mr. Smith said next time I'd better clean out my ears and the whole class laughed.
>
> **Mom:** (*Puts an arm around his shoulders to connect before giving him*

reassurance) I'm sorry that happened. Sometimes teachers forget how hard it is to be a kid. The good news is that no one in the class will even remember his comment by tomorrow. Do you want to sit down and have a snack together?

WHAT IF MY CHILD PUTS UP BARRIERS TO AFFECTION?

Building Block 2 involves showing affection, but showing affection to a child or teen who doesn't trust adults and doesn't feel worthy of love can be challenging. It's important to attune to the kind of affection your child can tolerate. They may need touch to be playful and brief. A side hug may be more comfortable than a full-on hug, and your child may tolerate more touch and affection when you're engaged in an activity together. Eye contact may feel threatening and may need to be very brief or avoided altogether. Your child or teen may accept a light rub of the shoulders or a gentle touch on the arm along with some affirming words, such as "It's all okay, we can handle this." Younger kids often enjoy a kiss on the top of the head as they go off to school or get tucked into bed.

You might have to look for and take advantage of those moments when your child is in their window of tolerance to actively show physical affection. On the other hand, there may be times when your child's nervous system is teetering on the edge of that window of tolerance and a little affection may help bring them back into their calm window.

Damien's uncle holds fast but attunes and shows affection to bring Damien back into the calm window:

Damien [age 10]: Can I have a brownie?

Uncle Earl: The brownies are for dessert.

Damien: But I can't wait! I'm starving, I'll die if I wait!

Uncle Earl: (*Places an arm around Damien affectionately and attunes* *while holding the boundary.*) I know it's really hard, Damien, but I also know you can do this. Dinner's almost ready. You're a strong kid. Can you help me stir this gravy here while I set the table? It'll make the time go by faster.

Damien: (*Grumbling*) I guess so.

Uncle Earl: I appreciate it, buddy.

Two activities that create affection and a more secure connection found in the clinician's manual, *EMDR and Family Therapy: Integrative Treatment for Attachment Trauma in Children* (Wesselmann, 2025), are the "Messages of Love" activity and the "Magical Cord of Love" activity. The activities will look a little different in your home than when they're used more formally in the therapy office but either way can create feelings of connection for your child or teen.

Messages of Love

Messages of love are positive reflections that will help your child feel close, loved, and connected. You can drop in some messages of love anywhere, any time. For example, you might drop them into a conversation in the car, or you might drop them into conversation at bedtime or morning time. If your child has avoidant tendencies and has a hard time taking in good things, just drop in one or two messages of love at a time.

To help you provide messages of love for your child, make some notes:

1. What are some early happy memories with your child or teen? When did your feelings of love first "grow" in your heart? Write down memories that come to you. If your son/daughter was born to you, jot down some positive memories about the pregnancy, birth, and early years.

   _____

   _____

   _____

   _____

   _____

41

2. What positive experiences have you and your child or teen shared, such as family vacations, building a snowman, playing favorite games, or attending movies or sporting events?

_____

_____

_____

_____

_____

3. What characteristics do you and your child or teen have in common (e.g., sense of humor, artistic, musical, athletic, love for animals)?

_____

_____

_____

_____

_____

4. What activities do you most enjoy doing with your child or teen?

_____

_____

_____

_____

_____

5. What attributes does your child or teen have that you enjoy?

_____

_____

_____

_____

_____

6. What hopes and dreams do you have for your child's future or for your future relationship with your child or teen?

_____

_____

_____

_____

_____

7. List recent or past triumphs your child or teen has achieved. Even small things are important. Example: "He put his clothes in the hamper without being asked."

_____

_____

_____

_____

_____

8. Make a list of things you would like to do with/for your child or teen if they were an infant again.

_____

_____

_____

_____

_____

Magical Cord of Love

Kids with a history of attachment trauma lack a sense that love is continuous. With your younger child you can say,

> We can't see love but it's real, right? It's like an invisible cord between my heart and your heart. I imagine it as a beautiful light. What color do you think it is? [*Child names a color.*] Yes, that sounds about right. I think it's magical, because no matter where you are and no matter where I am, you and I are always connected, heart to heart. Even if I get frustrated with you, the love cord is still there.

Once you introduce the idea, you can remind your child of the love cord when you drop them off at school or when you tuck them in at night. You can even tell your child you'll be sending them candies or hearts or teddy bears over the love cord throughout the day.

With your teen, you can say, "Remember, I'm thinking of you every day throughout the day, even though you're at school and I'm at home. Love is ongoing, like an invisible cord between us that connects us no matter what."

Zeah's mom sustains the connection through the cord of love:

(*Zeah's mom pulls up in front of the school.*)

Zeah: I don't want to go. Let's go back home.

Mom: (*Feels frustrated but takes a breath and attunes*) Zeah, honey, can you help me understand what's going on?

Zeah: I'm glad for Ms. Taylor that she had a baby, but we're going to have the substitute for 6 whole weeks. I don't like Mr. Baxter. His voice is scary.

Mom: I understand you feel nervous about Mr. Baxter. I'll bet some of the other kids are nervous, too. How about I send you some extra stuff on the magical cord of love today?

Zeah: What are you going to send me?

Mom: I'm going to send you candy hearts all morning long. And in the afternoon, I'm going to send you tiny teddy bears. I'll be thinking of you all day long.

Zeah: Okay.

Mom: How about I park and walk you up to the door today?

Strengthening Your Child's Sense of Safety and Connection With You

Mark a check by the activities you can engage in with your child or teen to build safety and connection:

☐ Pretend to paint each other's faces using a finger. Describe what colors and shapes you're using.

☐ Draw a letter or picture on your child's back with your finger.

Ask, "What do you think I made?" Then let your child take a turn to draw.

☐ Fix each other's hair or paint each other's nails. This is great with younger kids or teens.

☐ Brush your teeth together.

☐ Share a hobby or sport or a passion of yours with your child or teen.

☐ Play a board game or card game with your child or teen.

☐ Rock in a rocking chair or snuggle together.

☐ Spend time talking at bedtime or reading a book together. (Sometimes even teens enjoy having a story read to them.)

☐ Help your child or teen with chores for no reason.

☐ Occasionally, excuse them from chores and do something fun.

☐ Leave your child or teen sticky notes with positive affirmations or nurturing messages (e.g., "I had so much fun playing that game with you").

☐ Find a lotion (with a particular smell) that both you and your child enjoy, and rub it on your child's back, hands, or feet.

☐ Make up a family handshake that is special to your family.

☐ Point out positive behaviors, such as:
   • "I noticed you did a great job making your bed."
   • "I noticed you used your polite words today."

HOW CAN I PROVIDE SAFETY WHEN I DON'T FEEL SAFE?

Building Block 3 emphasizes the need for a safe and predictable environment for your child so they can decrease vigilance and self-protective defenses and experience a relaxed connection with you. The difficulty is that kids with a chaotic history often create a chaotic environment with their behaviors. You may feel as unsafe and anxious as your child does. Take a look to see if there's anything else that could be changed to add to a sense of safety and security in your home for both of you. Can you afford to hire some extra help in your home? Is there a volunteer organization that would help provide some respite? Do you have a friend who can come over and help you manage when you're anxious and stressed? Can you simplify your schedule, or ask family members or friends to assist with transporting kids to where they need to go? Is there chaos due to fighting between you and your partner or other family members? Don't put off seeking individual or couple therapy for stress and conflict. It can make all the difference in terms of establishing a safe environment for your child and for you.

What about routine and structure? Do you have a set of well-defined, reasonable house rules? Do you need to provide some incentives for following the rules? (You might skip ahead to Chapter 10 and read how to put an effective reward system in place.) Do you have an established routine for bedtime, morning time, homework time, and dinnertime? Despite their protests, kids crave a predictable routine they can depend upon.

HOW CAN I BE PLAYFUL WITH A CHILD OR TEEN WHO'S MOODY?

Building Block 4 emphasizes the need for shared pleasure in order to move your child or teen toward secure attachment. This can be challenging when kids have mood problems. The child or teen who didn't get to experience pleasure through playful connections when they were younger will lack adequate *feel good* chemicals. If your child's optimal window for learning how to play and connect was missed and replaced with experiences of loneliness, making up for these missed experiences will take time.

Hold on to your accepting, open, mentalizing demeanor and look for moments when there's an opportunity to be playful. Sometimes this may mean getting out a deck of cards or a board game, but other times it may be simply sharing an amusing story about yourself, telling a silly joke, or listening to your child's account of something funny that happened during the day. Following are some tips:

Tip 1: Stay Attuned by Staying Present

If you're playing together with your child or teen, turn off your cell phone and computer, and take the food off the stove. Your child needs your full attention and presence. When your cell phone dings and you begin texting, your child senses the disconnection.

Tip 2: Stay Attuned by Letting Your Child Take the Lead

By providing plenty of appropriate choices, you can let your child be in charge of the play while you follow their lead. Your child's play gives you a window into their world. Show interest by "noticing" and commenting or asking questions.

Four-year-old George and his mom color together:

Mom: What are you going to color, George?

George: I'm going to make a superhero.

Mom: I think I'll make a dog. I'll take that brown crayon. So what kind of powers does your superhero have?

George: He can turn into rubber and bounce really high.

Mom: Wow, I've never heard of a superhero who could do that. I like the way you're showing how he bounces by drawing those little curvy lines there. That's really creative! I would never think of that.

Tip 3: Be Aware That Your Child's Play Activities May Not Match Their Chronological Age

Because kids with a history of attachment trauma are often behind developmentally, your 12-year-old boy, for example, may want to play with a train set designed for a 6-year-old. He also might look more like a 6-year-old in the way he plays. He may have difficulty sharing, he may have a need to win, and he may ram trains and trucks together to make big noises. Your 14-year-old daughter might play with dolls meant for younger girls. If you meet your daughter at her level and play without judging, you'll connect with her and help her catch up with peers. She might have special dolls that no one else may touch. She might want to play "house" or "school." Don't force her to engage in play activities for which she is probably not ready. Some children naturally avoid engaging in immature play in front of peers, but other children are unaware of social ramifications.

Susan's mother communicates about a sensitive topic:

Susan's mother was afraid that Susan, who is 11 years old, would be teased by her peers at day care, so she spoke with Susan about the issue with sensitivity. The following vignette demonstrates her way of communicating with her daughter:

Mom: Susan, can I talk to you about something?

Susan: Sure.

Mom: This summer you'll be at the day care when I go back to work. I know how much you love playing with the toys that your younger sister plays with. I've let you take some of her toys that she doesn't care for anymore into your bedroom, and I think that it's just fine for you to play with them. You and I have even played together with those toys, right?

Susan: Yeah.

Mom: But I'm afraid that sometimes kids your age might make fun of other kids who play with those types of toys—even if maybe they secretly want to play with them, too. So let's talk about how you can play at the day care without attracting any teasing from the other kids.

Susan: They have lots of art supplies, maybe I could just paint and draw—and make things with clay.

Mom: I think that's a great idea.

Contrast the previous scene with this scene involving Grecian and his mom:

Mom: What do you have in that bag?

Grecian [age 9]: Five of my little stuffed animals. I want to bring them to day care today.

Mom: You can't bring those. In fact, we should throw those away. You're too big for them. Do you want people to think you're a baby?

Grecian: (*Starts to cry and runs to his room with his stuffed animals and slams the door*) You're mean! You hate my stuffed animals!

Mom: Knock it off right now!

Naturally, what follows is an argument that further reinforces Grecian's belief that it's not safe to trust his mother and that there's something wrong with him. Grecian's mother might have attuned to how much he loves his stuffed animals and then explained that there might be some kids at day care who would tease him for playing with stuffed animals, even though they might secretly play with stuffed animals at home. She might suggest playing with the animals after school and finding another toy to bring to school to make sure he has a good day.

Tip 4: Find Play You Both Enjoy

You're not a professional actor, and you can't convincingly pretend to enjoy an activity that you despise. Write down ideas you each like until you find several you both like. Relax, forget about the house or the yard work—it will wait. Laugh, joke, and keep it light.

Tip 5: Playtime Is Not Teaching Time

Don't quiz your child on math problems or colors. Don't ask your child to name things or spell things as you play. When you're playing, just play. Comment on what your child is doing, stay interested and attuned, joke, smile, and laugh. If you turn playtime into a "lesson," you move away from shared pleasure and fun, and it becomes a task.

Tip 6: If You Observe Your Child Reenacting Traumatic Experiences in Play, Share What You Observe With Your Child's Therapist

Many children reenact trauma in their play. Trauma play is the brain's way of attempting to gain mastery over terrifying memories. However, trauma play tends to get "stuck," and so the child repetitively repeats the same traumatic event in some form or other over and over again, without healthy resolution. If you observe your child engaging in this kind of play, let your child's therapist know. Your child's therapist can help your child move through the experience and integrate the "stuck" memory through therapy.

Tip 7: Incorporate Play in Your Daily Routines

Here are a few ideas to get you started. See if you can add some ideas of your own.

- Make silly faces for one another in the mirror while washing hands before dinner.
- Take turns reading from a riddle or joke book while sharing a snack after school.
- Play hand-clapping games while waiting for an appointment.
- Play "Rock, Paper, Scissors" while in line at the store.
- Play "I Spy" or "Twenty Questions" during trips in the car.
- _____
- _____
- _____

Make a list of times when your child or teen typically seems to be highly sensitive and reactive, such as getting up, driving to school, dinnertime, homework time, or bedtime:

_____
_____
_____
_____

Make a plan to purposefully connect at each of these times by snuggling, sharing a snack and talking, doing something playful, or talking about the "cord of love."

Tip 8: Conversation Starters for Mealtime or Car Time

Here are a few ideas to get you started. See if you can add some more of your own.

- If you could be any animal just for today, what animal would you be and why?
- If you could go anywhere in the world today, where would you go?
- If you could bring a superhero with you to school today, who would you bring?
- If you could have a superpower just for today, what superpower would you choose?
- If we could spend today in another country, what country would you choose and what would you want to do there?
- If one of your friends could become part of our family just for today, which friend would you choose?
- _____
  _____
  _____
  _____

MAKING REPAIRS IS HARD WHEN IT'S ALL UP TO YOU

Building Block 5, repairs, is critical to attachment security. In your other relationships, repairs are a two-way street. With friends or a partner, they apologize and you apologize. However, right now, your child or teen has little capacity for repairs on their part because their activated nervous system keeps them in survival mode where they lack the capacity to reflect in that way. Eventually, your connection with your child will help them develop the ability to think and reflect on the feelings of others and make repairs.

As you make repairs, you're demonstrating that you're trustworthy and you're role modeling the actions. Remember, you're in this for the long game. You'll see them following your lead over time.

In this vignette, Theresa's dad lets his emotions get the best of him and then initiates a repair:

Five-year-old Theresa is attempting to learn how to tie her shoes. She becomes frustrated, hurls the shoe across the room, and runs into her bedroom, slamming the door behind her.

Dad: Hey, there's no reason to slam this door or get angry. It's just a shoe, for heaven's sake. Forget about it!

Theresa: I hate myself! I hate everybody.

Dad: *(Voice getting louder.)* You're being ridiculous. Just stay in this room until you're finished acting up. And from now on, you're wearing Velcro!

Theresa: *(Cries and crawls under her covers.)*

Dad: *(Realizes he's dysregulated and creating a disconnect.)* Hold on, Theresa, I apologize. I should not be so cranky. Come sit with me. Will you forgive me? I can imagine learning to tie is frustrating. I should have been more helpful. Let's both take some deep breaths together, okay?

Theresa: *(Comes and sits next to dad.)* I don't like it when you yell.

Dad: I'll bet I hurt your feelings, didn't I? *(Theresa nods.)* I don't want to hurt your feelings. You're really important to me. I'll work on my yelling, okay?

Theresa: Okay.

Dad: And you know, it's always okay to ask me to help you with stuff. Let's see if I can help you with this business of tying your shoes.

In the following vignette, David's grandfather misattunes, then corrects course and makes a repair:

David [age 14]: *(Comes in the door after school and throws his backpack)* I hate this school and everybody in it!

Grandpa: You don't hate them. You're just tired. Go lie down on your bed for a while.

David: You don't know anything!

Grandpa: Hmm, you're right. I apologize, I don't actually know what's going on. Why don't you come and have a piece of this homemade bread with me, and then you can help me understand.

In this vignette, 10-year-old Juan hurt a classmate at school. Juan's dad gets angry and then corrects course and makes a repair:

Dad: Juan, I just received a call from your teacher. You poked another student in the back with a sharp edge of a ruler. You have a detention every day this week. (*Begins to yell*) I'm furious with you right now. Why would you do that? What's wrong with you?

Juan stares at the floor and shrugs his shoulders. Juan's dad takes a quick walk outside and calms himself down. He remembers the new strategies and rejoins Juan.

Dad: (*Touching Juan's shoulder lightly*) Look, I apologize for yelling. That was wrong. I got too worked up. (*Juan shrugs.*) Juan, let's see if we can figure this out. Can you help me understand what was going on today?

Juan: I just got so mad. I hate her. She's always laughing at me.

Dad: (*Nodding*) I don't like it when people laugh at me, either. Does it hurt your feelings?

Juan: Yeah, I guess. And it's embarrassing.

Dad: Okay, yeah, I get that. That's hard. But you know, poking with a ruler still isn't okay.

Juan: I know.

Dad: You know, whenever you're having a problem with someone—or with anything—you can come to me. So let's sit down and do some problem solving about this situation, okay?

Juan: Okay.

By getting himself back into a mentalizing state and making a repair with Juan, Dad was able to invite Juan to collaborate in exploring the problem. This turned the whole episode into a learning experience for Juan.

Leo's parents make a repair when they realized they'd let their fighting get out of hand:

Jacinda and Ralph were fighting a great deal over how to handle their financial problems. They realized that the environment was not safe and predictable, and that this was likely hurting their 8-year-old son, Leo. Leo's therapist encouraged them to acknowledge this with Leo, attune to his feelings, and make a repair.

> **Ralph:** Leo, I know things have been stressful at home. You've probably heard your mom and me arguing over the bills lately, haven't you, buddy?
>
> **Leo:** I don't know.
>
> **Jacinda:** Leo, we're so sorry. We don't mean to upset you. Our arguments are not okay. Dad and I still love each other. We're just stressed.
>
> **Ralph:** We're going to work on it, but also, you can tell us if we're messing up and making you feel unsafe, okay?
>
> **Leo:** (*Nodding*) Okay.

Moving your child toward attachment security is not an all-or-nothing thing. Each time your child gets to experience a little moment of safe connection with you, their nervous system gets to relax just a bit more and they're pulled just a bit closer toward a sense of trust and security.

ATTUNING TO HIDDEN FEELINGS ABOUT DIFFERENCES (ETHNICITY, DISABILITIES, SEXUAL/GENDER ISSUES)

We all want to feel like we're a match, like we belong in our family, in our neighborhood, and in the larger community. Bringing kids and families together is always a good thing, but adoption does lead to children having differing backgrounds and ethnicity from their parents or siblings. Other differences kids worry about include any differences in physical appearance from the rest of the family or differences created by a medical issue, a weight issue, or a disability. Kids are sensitive to differences no matter what the cause. Many kids who are different in some way from others experience bullying and rejection from their peer group, which can be deeply traumatizing. Kids become convinced they'll never belong or they're not as good as others.

Sometimes parents believe that if they don't say anything about the child's differences, it won't be a problem. The truth is quite the opposite. Not mentioning the differences doesn't erase the distress but it does make kids think it's not okay to bring it up. When parents avoid the topic of their differences, it may even cause the child or teen to believe their differences are too shameful to talk about. If you haven't broached the topic, you can bring it up by letting your child or teen know that you love everything about them and that we all have characteristics that differ from others around us, which is a good thing because diversity makes us more interesting. Let them know that you're aware, however, that some kids and even some adults can at times be critical of characteristics that are different from their own. You might help them make sense of it by explaining that those who put others down are trying to make themselves feel bigger or more powerful because deep down, those individuals feel insecure about themselves. Emphasize that the mean words or actions of others are of no consequence to your child's worthiness. At the same time, attune and empathize with your child's feelings of hurt, because no explanations will make their hurt magically disappear.

If your child or teen has a different ethnic background than other members of the family, find ways to learn more and honor their heritage. Help your child get involved in school groups or church groups that have members who share your child's ethnicity or culture. Explore the food, the history, and the religion related to the heritage of each child in your family.

Many kids, biological as well as foster or adopted kids, struggle with differences related to sexuality or gender identity. As they enter puberty, many kids may find themselves attracted to other kids of the same gender. Some kids are recognizing that their gender identity doesn't match their gender at birth. Lots of parents end up struggling with complicated feelings of their own when their kids disclose these types of issues, yet the child who's disclosed needs immediate reassurance that they're loved and worthy. If you discover your child is struggling in this area and you're feeling overwhelmed, spend some one-on-one time with your child's therapist or your own therapist to work through your own emotions so you can provide your child or teen with the support they need.

ATTUNING TO THE HIDDEN PROBLEM OF DISSOCIATION

We all dissociate in a mild way occasionally. When we leave our window of tolerance and move into sympathetic nervous system activation, it's easy for any of us, if we get overloaded, to move into dorsal vagal shutdown and zone out mentally for a few moments. Kids who experienced a number of traumatic experiences when they were very young sometimes exhibit regular patterns of dissociation when they're anxious or triggered. The automatic dissociative response is the nervous system's way of helping the young child escape a difficult situation. As they get older, they may continue to dissociate by going blank, staring into space, or retreating into their own fantasy world. This can be confused with attention deficit disorder (ADD), which causes kids to be highly distractible and lose focus when they're supposed to be concentrating and learning.

Kids who have strong feelings related to earlier traumas may dissociate by stepping into the feelings and perceptions that were present at the time of the trauma. Because their feelings are connected to a time when they were younger, they may lose access to their present-day thoughts and feelings. Because they've been triggered by some kind of reminder of their traumas they regress and step into their younger state. They may use childish language, curl up in a ball, suck their fingers, or wet their pants. Sometimes dissociation in kids involves sudden unexpected behaviors that seem to come out of nowhere and don't match the situation, like extreme silliness, aggressive episodes or meltdowns, or imitating an animal. Kids who exhibit dissociative episodes related to triggers don't do this on purpose. It's important to note that dissociation is not intentional, and your child or teen can't control it.

Immature behaviors that don't match the child's age may also be related to developmental deficits caused by chronic trauma, FASD, or ASD. The difference is that regression caused by dissociation is temporary, while immature behaviors caused by delayed development are constant.

A rare condition is full-blown dissociative identity disorder (DID). In this case, the child has quick changes in their state with behaviors that aren't typical, along with loss of memory for the episode. They may refer to themselves by a different name or use a different voice. Sometimes parents think the dissociative child has an evil part or bad part. This message can be very damaging for a child. There are no evil or bad parts, even when dissociative episodes involve aggression. Punishing episodes involving dissociation will increase fear and increase the dissociative response.

Therapy with a provider experienced in working with dissociation is crucial. Whether the child has DID or just a pattern of regressing or going away mentally, the therapist will work to strengthen the child's most mature state and keep the child's most mature state in the office. The therapist won't ask to talk to parts or states directly or give them names or emphasize the separateness of parts. Instead, the therapist using the EMDR and family model will encourage the most mature child self to reassure the younger parts of self on the inside (Wesselmann, 2025). The therapist will help the child learn how to tuck younger parts of the child into safe places through gentle visualizations. The brain of the child or teen is still developing, and the therapist's goal is to calm the brain's dissociative tendencies, not strengthen them.

Strengthening the child's most mature state helps integrate the child's internal system.

The most effective way you can respond to signs of dissociation is to increase your child's sense of safe connection with you. A light touch and/or some reassuring words that remind them of your supportive presence can help. For example, you might say,

> Hey, sweetie, I think something's made you really anxious. Remember you're right here with me. I'm here to help with whatever's going on. Remember what a great kid you are and how smart you are. Remember how big you are and how old you are now. Remember all the people who love you and keep you safe today.

What your child or teen needs more than anything to combat dissociation is connection and co-regulation from you to feel grounded, safe, and loved.

ATTUNING TO HIDDEN GRIEF

If you're raising a biological child with attachment trauma, your child may have grief related to the loss of the other parent in the case of death or a separation or grief related to other losses in the family. If you're not the biological parent, your child may be suffering from the deep emotional pain associated with "ambiguous loss," as described in Chapter 2. Your child may have no way to articulate or make peace with grief for birth parents they know are alive but are unknown to them in terms of their whereabouts or their well-being. Your child may be struggling to develop a sense of their roots and identity with all the missing pieces of their life.

Your child may have also lost grandparents, pets, toys, classmates, and other important pieces of their early life during moves and separations. Even kids adopted in infancy will experience complicated feelings of sadness, rejection, hurt, abandonment, and confusion related to early separations and losses.

With kids, grief often goes unrecognized. It drives oppositional behaviors and meltdowns that seem unprovoked. They may engage in self-soothing behaviors, such as stealing, hoarding, overeating, or masturbating. Attuning to your child's grief and providing emotional support, understanding, and physical affection will help your child get "unstuck" and perhaps cry or talk, allowing them to move through their grief. They'll find comfort and gradual acceptance through their connection with you.

When you recognize that your child may be feeling sad related to losses, connect physically and emotionally. A very young child will benefit from rocking with you in a rocking chair, because rocking adds additional comfort and helps bring about emotional release. Invite your older child to sit close on the couch. With an adolescent who resists physical closeness, reach out with a light touch on the hand or shoulder. I find that the best words to say when kids are sad are "I'm so sorry for the sad things that have happened" and "All your feelings are okay, I'm here for you." Parents are often surprised at the difference attunement, compassion, and touch can make in their child's ability to open up their heart.

Martha attunes to Janie's hidden grief:

Martha described how connecting and attuning helped her work through a period of acute grief with her 3-year-old niece, Janie, whose mother was incarcerated:

> I had taken Janie to the park, and she was being a terrible pill. Here we were, at the swings and the slides, her favorite place, and suddenly she started hitting me for no reason and shouting, "You're stupid." At first, I lost my temper a little bit. I raised my voice and said, "Janie, knock it off. I came here to make you happy. We'll just go home if that's what you want." I picked her up and carried her, screaming and kicking, to the car. I was really frustrated, and I looked back to see if everyone was staring at us, and then it hit me. All the other kids were there playing with their moms, while Janie was there with her old auntie. I knew then that Janie was feeling grief about her mom, like you had pointed out. So I remembered what you told me about holding

her and telling her I'm sorry and all that. I sat down on a bench and started just rocking with her, side to side, over and over. I put my cheek next to hers, and I just kept saying, "I'm so sorry, Janie. I'm so sorry about your mommy. I'm so sorry. I love you, it's okay. All your feelings are okay. It's okay to be sad, I'll help you."

Then Janie just burst into tears, and she cried and cried and hung onto me. It just broke my heart. But after about a half hour, she settled down, and do you know? We went back to the slides, and she played and had fun. I am just so thankful you taught me about this, because otherwise I might have just gone and punished her, and all those feelings would have stayed stuck inside of her causing more and more problems. I know this will happen again and again, but I will know now what to do.

Many foster or adoptive parents have feelings of anger toward their child's birth parents, sometimes due to choices the birth parents made. It's important to reflect upon your own feelings and process your feelings through your own support system so they don't get in the way of attuning to the grief and loss experienced by your child. Keep in mind that children grieve the loss of their birth parents no matter how they were treated in the birth home, or when their placement was changed. Some parents are tempted to invalidate their child's sadness, reminding their child of the poor functioning of their biological parents. This gives kids the impression their feelings are bad and must be kept secret, which throws up roadblocks to closeness and connection with their present parents.

ATTUNING TO YOUR CHILD'S DEVELOPMENTAL DEFICITS

Trauma during important stages of development throws kids off course and leaves them with important social, emotional, and cognitive deficits. Whenever your child's nervous system was firing due to traumatic circumstances in their earlier life, the regions of your child's brain designed for integrating information, learning, and maturing were shut down. Your child may have missed out on learning skills such as how to listen to others, how to articulate and cope with feelings and thoughts, and how to compromise, problem solve, focus, memorize, organize, and communicate. Your child may have missed out on learning practical day-to-day skills and routines related to using the toilet, brushing their teeth, getting ready for bed, getting ready for the day, eating meals, picking up their things, and managing their time.

Parents of kids with developmental deficits or brain-based challenges often fail to recognize where their child is missing skills or lacking in appropriate habits due to trauma during critical periods of maturation. Identifying your child's deficits can help you focus on providing the teaching and assistance they need.

If your child is a teenager, you'll be happy to know that adolescence is not the end of brain development. Although your adolescent's brain won't become bigger, the neural connections will continue to develop until age 25 or even a few years beyond that. As you build trust and connection, you'll be able to assist your child with overcoming some of those deficits through the use of teachable moments and coaching your child through stuck places.

Some kids have deficits due to brain-based challenges caused by exposure to substances in utero as described in Chapter 2. Kids on the autism spectrum, kids with ADHD, and kids with other types of learning disabilities have deficits in learning and managing day-to-day challenges that are inherent to the neurodivergent brain. Although symptoms related to their trauma can resolve, kids with brain-based challenges will always have brain differences. (See Chapter 6 for guidance on helping kids with brain-based challenges.)

Yvonne's mother has unrealistic expectations but makes a repair:
Mom told 10-year-old Yvonne to pick up her room and get herself organized for school the next day. Yvonne had joined the family through adoption 2 years earlier. She peeked her head in and

found Yvonne sitting on the floor sorting a deck of cards into a pile of red cards and a pile of black cards:

> **Mom:** Yvonne, I told you to pick up your room and get organized for school. You've been in here for an hour and the room is still a mess. That's it. No bedtime snack for you.
>
> **Yvonne:** (*Throwing her deck of cards*) That's no fair! I've been working on my room for an hour!
>
> **Mom:** Oh really? You've been sitting there playing with cards. You haven't done a thing in here.
>
> **Yvonne:** I was organizing my cards! That takes a long time! And before that, I put clothes on all my Barbie dolls and lined them up on the bed!
>
> **Mom:** (*Attuning and repairing*) Okay, I understand now. I'm sorry, Yvonne, I shouldn't have lost my temper. I can see that you need some help learning how to do this. How about I pick up along with you and show you the best way to get this done? I think a good way to go is to start by picking up and putting away the things that are lying on the floor.
>
> **Yvonne:** Okay, I guess.
>
> **Mom:** I have an idea! Let's make it more fun. What's your favorite color?
>
> **Yvonne:** Pink.
>
> **Mom:** That's right! Okay, let's see how fast we can pick up all the pink items to start!

Helping your child make up for social and emotional deficits requires holding on to a mentalizing state and creating connection through attunement, safety, and playfulness to calm your child's nervous system and activate trust. Stay matter-of-fact and avoid lecturing or shaming your child or teen. Show them instead of telling them what to do whenever possible. Invite your child to work on getting things done along with you. Be playful and light-hearted as much as you can. By avoiding shame and keeping a pleasant, caring demeanor, you'll find your child will be much more cooperative and motivated. If your child feels embarrassed, ashamed, or demeaned, they're likely to move outside their window of tolerance for the task and into a fight-or-flight or shut-down zone.

Note About School

 Although your child or teen may benefit from some homework help, don't confuse helping them in areas where they have developmental deficits with micromanaging their homework or placing too much emphasis on school achievement. Don't set expectations for high grades, prioritize grades, or take responsibility for your child's grades. Remember that your child's grades are not a reflection of you or your parenting methods, and they are far less important than your child's sense of safety, security, and self-worth when it comes to getting along in life. Your child needs emotional closeness with you above all else.

 If you're pulling your hair out trying to help your child or teen through homework for hours each night, or if homework time is triggering meltdowns, it's time to advocate for them to receive the testing and full school accommodations they need. The homework that is sent home should be a match for your child's developmental level. The time your child spends on homework should be reasonable, with ample downtime for relaxing or interacting with family or friends. Homework that is appropriate to your child's needs will allow your child to build confidence, not tear it down.

Chapter 5

Co-Regulation:
It's a Big Job, but Someone Has to Do It!

LITERALLY. SOMEONE HAS TO DO IT. Poor regulation is a major developmental deficit for kids with a history of attachment trauma. All kids need co-regulation help from their parents, but the need is much greater in general for kids with a narrow window of tolerance.

Think about a time that your child or teen was agitated, argumentative, or angry over some minor situation and consider Figure 1.2 in Chapter 1. When your child's window of tolerance is narrow, small everyday events feel big, again and again. If that weren't enough, your child's capacity for reaching out is poor due to lack of trust. Their nervous system is constantly on fire and lighting up your nervous system the way one sparkler can light another sparkler on the Fourth of July. Ordering them to stop their behavior doesn't work. Yelling and punishing doesn't work.

THE CO-REGULATING DEMEANOR

You have the power to co-regulate your child when your child feels a sense of safety in your presence. Your general demeanor is all-important to the task. You transmit safety through a relaxed facial expression, body posture, and voice tone, as well as words that convey attunement and affection. If you sense your child will be receptive, you may be able to reach out and connect through a gentle touch on the shoulder or a hug.

Magic on Your Child's Brain

Think of every problem behavior as a potential opportunity to learn more about the emotions and upset thoughts with which your child or teen is struggling. The building blocks of attunement and affection can act like magic on your child's brain. When you notice that your child is "revving up," step into your mentalizing state and show affection through a touch on the shoulder or a little side hug, invite them to sit by you for a bit, and provide some reassuring words. Following separations, even for a few hours, take time to connect through attunement, affection, or playfulness to strengthen their sense of security and trust. Just a few moments of time are all it takes to "tether" your child and help them become regulated in a way that benefits their nervous system *and* wards off problem behaviors.

Remember, too, that you cannot help your child all alone. Your child's therapist(s) will be working on calming your child's brain in therapy.

Practice Makes Perfect (or Close Enough)

The best time to help your child learn to calm their brain is when they're already calm. As you connect with your child at bedtime and you notice that they're finally relaxed and calm, you can share what you notice and help them become aware of how pleasurable it feels.

Scott's mom uses bedtime for co-regulation and connection to help Scott develop trust and a calmer nervous system overall:

Mom: Do you want me to rub your back a little after I tuck you in?

Scott [age 6]: Yes, and can you tell me a little story?

Mom: (*Tells Scott a little story while she rubs his back*) You look all cozy and relaxed. Don't you just love your cozy, warm bed? You're all relaxed, your body is relaxed, your brain is relaxed and calm . . . it's like you're just floating on a beautiful cloud, with nowhere you have to go, just sailing along, easily . . . it feels so cozy, relaxing, easy. . . .

CO-REGULATION WHEN YOUR CHILD'S NERVOUS SYSTEM IS FIRING

Right now, your child or teen is likely overwhelmed by many different feelings driven by many different triggers and a memory network full of trauma with little capacity to recognize or articulate what's happening on the inside. No wonder their emotions are being expressed through challenging behaviors!

When your child's nervous system is lighting up and they're leaving their window of tolerance for the distress, their voice volume and their words ramp up. They may start stomping, slamming doors, and throwing objects. They may become suddenly hyperactive. They may start arguing, sassing, using bad words, whining or crying, or become aggressive with their siblings or friends.

The first and most critical step for co-regulating your child's nervous system when they're moving into the fight-or-flight zone is regulating your own internal state. Just as we have a visceral response when a car alarm or a smoke alarm sounds, we tend to have an automatic, gut response to the screams of a child or sassing of a teenager. If our actions and words are driven by our gut response, they'll definitely not be coming from a place of mentalization and reflection. If our face and voice exhibit our anger, our child's sympathetic nervous system will be ignited.

By taking a few seconds to pause and check in with ourselves, we can give ourselves time to breathe and grab hold of a mentalizing state. We can soften our face and our voice tone. We can relax our posture. We can change impending disaster to an opportunity for building connection and reflection. Remember the keys to a mentalizing approach include acceptance and an openness to whatever your child may wish to show you or tell you.

As you attune to your child or teen with no demands or expectations for "pulling it together" in a certain time period, your child feels a sense of connection and trust and their nervous system will calm in response to your own calm nervous system. The co-regulation will widen their window of tolerance for their emotions and make it possible for your child or teen to notice and put words to their feelings and collaborate with you to solve problems.

To attune to your child's emotions, you may not need many words. Avoid using words that indicate you're the expert on your child's emotions and behaviors. Avoid, for example, words like "I can see that you're mad. If you would just think about it, you'd see there's no reason to be mad."

Instead, co-regulate through attunement and empathy. You might say, "Hey, I can see you're having a hard time. Can we sit together for a minute? Let's just take a minute to breathe." When your child sees a calm, empathic expression on your face and hears an understanding voice tone, their social engagement system starts to flicker just a bit. As their nervous system co-regulates with your calm nervous system, their emotions don't seem as dire.

Later, when the timing is right, you might say, "I'd like to understand more about what you were feeling earlier. Could we talk about it a little bit?" Later, you may be able to talk together about the trigger and problem solve to help them manage better the next time. You might ask, "If that happens again, do you want to go into your room to calm down or would you rather sit with me and take some deep breaths with me? Are there some words I could say that would help?"

Keep in mind that once your child goes into a full-blown meltdown, they have no access to their thinking brain and there's no way to engage in reciprocal communication. Chapter 7 describes the best way to manage the three phases of a major meltdown that has passed the "point of no return."

Eleven-year-old Cindy and her dad work together to make a plan for preventing meltdowns:

Dad: Cindy, that meltdown was no fun for either you or me this morning. Can we figure out some things that might help the meltdowns go away?

Cindy: (*Feels ashamed and puts her head under her pillow*)

Dad: I know it's hard to talk about, but I just want to help. I was thinking maybe we could figure out a safe, calm place where you could go to help you calm down when your brain starts getting upset. We could put some special things in your calm place to help you.

Cindy: How about my bedroom?

Dad: Sure, that would be fine. What do you think could help you calm down while you are in your room?

Cindy: I think it might calm me to lie down on my bed with all my stuffed animals and my blanket.

Dad: That's a good idea. Do you want Mom or me to go in there with you?

Cindy: Yes, could you just sit on my bed without talking?

Dad: Sure, we can do that.

Notice that Cindy's dad doesn't reinforce her shame. He instead reduces her shame through a nonjudgmental, matter-of-fact, problem-solving approach.

Children need to feel safe and understood to pay attention to what they're feeling and express themselves. Reassure your child that you love them and that all their feelings are normal, not bad.

Brain Talk in Action

Once we've built some trust and connection with our kids through the building blocks and a mentalizing state, we can sometimes teach and encourage skills to help them begin learning how to calm themselves. For example, if you find your child or teen is receptive, you may be able to offer to take some deep breaths with them as a step toward helping them learn to use breathing for regulation. You may be able to massage their shoulders a bit and suggest they drop their shoulders to release tension in their body for self-calming. You may even be able to teach them some self-talk using child-friendly language. For example, you can suggest they use their smart thinking brain to talk to the nervous part of their brain. You might want to coach them a bit as to what the smart thinking part of their brain can say to the upset part of their brain. Attune and look for times when your child seems connected and receptive. This kind of teaching and coaching should never be forced.

Terry's dad helps Terry with self-talk:

Terry, age 14, was planning to attend a 2-day overnight basketball camp away from home. Because of his emotional and social delays, this was the first time he would attend something like this since he was adopted at age 7. Like many kids with a history of attachment trauma, he didn't think of talking to his parents about his anxiety but he was visibly agitated the day prior to leaving for camp:

Dad: Terry, why don't we sit out on the porch for a bit while Mom is fixing dinner? You know it would be very, very normal to feel nervous about going to camp. This is your first camp away, and lots of kids get a little nervous about that. Do you think you might be feeling a little nervous?

Terry: Yeah, maybe.

Dad: Remember how we can use our smart thinking brain up here in the front part of our head (*pointing*) to talk to the nervous downstairs part of our brain? I wonder what your smart thinking brain might tell the nervous part of your brain?

Terry: Um, everything's okay?

Dad: Sure, you can talk to the nervous part of your brain and say, "Everything's okay." You might say, "I'll be with my good buddies, Sam and Dave. I met the coaches, and they're really nice. And it's just for 2 days, and it's only a half hour away. If I needed anything important, my parents would be there in a jiffy." Do you think you can tell your brain all that?

Terry: Yeah, okay.

Helping Your Child With Problem-Focused Coping

If any of us experience some distress and are unable to tolerate it enough to step back and reflect and think about what to do, we may move into the fight-or-flight zone and unthinkingly do whatever we need to do to get rid of our distress or protect ourselves. If we feel like eating a carton of ice cream to feel better, we eat the carton of ice cream. If we feel like yelling at someone, we yell at someone. If we feel like shutting down, we shut down. This all happens immediately and automatically.

If we can tolerate that distress and mentalize a bit, we can find the space we need to make a better decision. Unfortunately, the maladaptive coping style is the default for kids with a narrow window of tolerance and quick dysregulation due to trauma.

If I'm engaged in *maladaptive coping* . . .

1. I feel distressed.
2. I can't tolerate it and my nervous system fires up.
3. I'll do whatever my nervous system tells me to do to self-protect or get rid of the feelings.

If we know our feelings won't actually hurt us, and we know feelings come and go and they're normal, we're less panicked by our own feelings. Our window of tolerance is a good size, and that allows us to think. We can notice and identify our feelings, identify the cause, and consider whether we need to just accept things as they are or whether there's a problem we need to fix. We can also consider reaching out for help. This is called problem-focused coping. It comes naturally only if we had someone attuned and supporting us with emotions when we were young. Otherwise, we have to develop needed skills, expand our window of tolerance, and become intentional about coping with our feelings and mentalizing the situation.

If I'm engaged in *problem-focused coping* . . .

1. I feel distressed.
2. I tolerate the feelings, and I mentalize.

I accept the situation, solve the problem, or reach out for help. As you practice co-regulation with your child, your attuned presence will gradually build trust and connection. Your child may become receptive to your help with developing skills for problem-focused coping.

Jamei's aunt helps him with skills for problem-focused coping:

Jamei, age 13, came home from his friend's house and began kicking the sofa.

Aunt Kea: Jamei, whatever's happened, it will be okay. Help me understand.

Jamei: I went over there, and all Paulo wanted to do was text on his phone. He started texting a girl and he kept saying, "Just a minute, just a minute." I gave up and came home.

Aunt Kea: I'd be frustrated. Is that what you're feeling?

Jamei: (*Stops kicking the couch*) Yeah.

Aunt Kea: (*Nodding*) That's a normal feeling. I don't like it when I'm frustrated, but at least it doesn't last forever, and I know the feeling can't hurt me. Can we sit down here and take some deep breaths? (*Jamei shrugs and takes a few breaths.*) You look calmer, now, Jamei. So let's do some problem solving. Could you set some ground rules with Paulo?

Jamei: Maybe I could tell him we need to make an agreement about what we're going to do before we get together.

Aunt Kea: That's a really good idea. It may work. Can we also think about what you could do if he breaks the agreement? Because we can't control other people, and people do make mistakes.

Jamei: I guess I could just come home if he breaks the agreement. Maybe call a different friend?

Aunt Kea: That's one idea. Or do you suppose you could just make the best of the situation and play one of his video games while he's on his phone?

Jamei: Yeah, I guess.

Aunt Kea: Okay, so now you know you have some options. Hey, thanks for letting me help you think this through.

Jamei: Sure.

It's not easy to stay calm and connected when your child is having a hard time. But setting a daily intention is well worth it. Over time, you'll see the difference it makes—in your child, in you, and in your connection.

Chapter 6

Prenatal Substance Exposure, Autism, and Attention-Deficit/Hyperactivity Disorder

Your child or teen is a unique combination of innate talents and strengths as well as emotional and neurobiological challenges caused by attachment trauma. Some children with a difficult history have additional inborn brain differences, such as ASD or ADHD. Some kids have brain differences caused by prenatal substance exposure.

The idea that there may be additional factors impacting your child's functioning may feel overwhelming. However, recognizing their differences gives you a more complete picture and helps you help your child. It's important to remember that kids with brain challenges also carry unique strengths and talents that should be nurtured and celebrated.

BRAIN CHALLENGES RELATED TO AUTISM, ADHD, AND LEARNING DISABILITIES

Autism, ADHD, and learning disabilities are forms of neurodivergence. Neurodivergence means the structure and functioning of the brain differs in important ways from the majority of the population. Kids can have one or more forms of neurodivergence in addition to a history of attachment trauma.

Autism

Autism is a form of neurodivergence. Autism is on a spectrum, as characteristics associated with autism can vary widely from one child to the next. Kids on the autism spectrum may speak well, may have great difficulty with communication, or may not speak at all. Some may feel things intensely while others struggle to notice their emotions. Some kids with ASD may have stimming behaviors (self-stimulation for self-regulation), such as hand flapping, scratching, rocking, or vocalizing, and others may not. Kids with ASD may have trouble paying attention to some things while they hyperfocus on things they like. Some may be extremely concrete while others are capable of discussing abstract ideas. Some kids with ASD struggle a great deal with reading social cues and understanding the nuances of interactions, and others may struggle less. They often have either severe or mild difficulty managing sensory stimulation from sound, taste, touch, or smells. Often eye contact is overstimulating.

Because kids with ASD hyperfocus on things they enjoy, they often become very skilled at those things. Many kids with ASD are highly intelligent and have excellent memory and attention to detail. Science, technology, and math are often strong suits. Many grow up to become very successful in their area of expertise.

When adults expect autistic children to change their neurological functioning to conform to society's standards, the unrealistic expectations commonly create feelings of alienation and low self-esteem, leading to secondary mood and behavioral disorders. When their family, school, and community accept and accommodate the ways in which they interact with the world, they can function at their best.

In past years, many professionals and parents attempted to eradicate stimming behaviors in autistic children through behavioral methods. Some professionals also forced eye contact and physical closeness. As the children grew older, they informed their parents and professionals that those methods were not helpful and were actually harmful and traumatizing. Because autistic individuals have been able to give this feedback, our society has advanced in that we know the importance of accepting their brain differences. Applied behavior analysis (ABA) therapy is a behavioral therapy that can be a helpful therapy as long as the provider is respectful of neurodivergent traits, sensitive to the child's emotions, highlighting their strengths, and applying rewards versus punishments. The approach is long term and treats behaviors, not traumatic stress.

Attention-Deficit/Hyperactivity Disorder

Another form of neurodivergence is ADHD. Typical symptoms include hyperactivity, impulsivity, and trouble paying attention, although some kids are distractible without the hyperactivity (ADD). The ADHD symptoms are caused by slow electrical activity in the prefrontal brain, leaving the child or teen with impaired capacity to manage impulses, focus, stay on task, delay gratification, think through their actions, or solve problems. Whereas adults often assume the ADHD child or teen is choosing to be noncompliant with tasks, the truth is, they're not able to function like kids who are neurotypical. Like children who are autistic, they're trying to fit into a world that is not a match for their brain differences. And let's not forget, we're focusing on kids who also have challenges imposed by attachment trauma and its impact on their emotions, brain structure, and nervous system.

Other forms of neurodivergence include learning disabilities related to reading, handwriting, spelling, math, eye–hand coordination, and sense of direction. Many kids have multiple forms of neurodivergence.

Kids with ADHD and/or learning disabilities often think outside the box and are highly creative. They may excel at music, dance, drama, art, or sports. Fostering your child's gifts is an important way to help them develop a positive self-concept.

Testing

An evaluator who has expertise in assessing neurodivergence, as well as co-occurring mental health problems and trauma symptoms, can help differentiate symptoms inherent to the child's neurology and symptoms caused by past attachment trauma. Some problems may have more than one cause. Testing results can help you view your child's behaviors through all the correct lenses to help give you a clear picture of your child's capacities. Understanding your child's brain differences will help you become more attuned to their challenges and strengths and build greater attachment security through empathy and encouragement.

Medication

Discussion of medications is beyond the scope of this book, but medications may indeed be helpful for your child's mood problems and attentional problems. The brain differences can make it difficult for prescribers to find the most effective medications, so find someone with the appropriate expertise.

Often parents want their kids to learn skills to manage their ADHD without medication. The problem is that significant symptoms indicate slow activity in the prefrontal brain, which leaves kids with diminished capacity to focus, think, delay gratification, and problem solve. Expecting kids to control those functions is like expecting them to row a boat without oars. The child ends up the recipient of irritation, anger, and criticism from adults and rejection from their peers. Living with an untreated ADHD brain can be traumatic for the child, which complicates recovery from earlier traumatic experiences. When kids can get on the proper ADHD medication, essential circuits in their prefrontal brain light up, giving them improved capacity to manage their symptoms. Their brain won't function exactly like the neurotypical brain and they'll still need accommodations, but they'll manage much better and feel better.

AT-HOME ACCOMMODATIONS

Just as accommodations help kids with autism or ADHD feel best and do best at school, accommodations at home can help them function better in the family. Accommodating kids at home means attuning to their challenges and adjusting expectations to match what they can and can't do. It means helping them function through supervision, structure, and predictable routines. With accommodations in place, there's less stress and more room for building relationships. Remember, we're talking about kids with neurodivergence *and* a history of attachment trauma. The building blocks for secure attachment are crucial to your overall success in helping your child manage their symptoms. Staying calm, attuned, affectionate, and playful in your interactions will make all the difference in terms of building a sense of trust and closeness for your child.

Incentives may help motivate your child or teen to stay on task moment to moment, as long as what you're asking them to do is not unrealistic and the incentives are immediate. For example, a little extra time on a video game after dinner can be an incentive for staying seated at dinner. An extra bedtime story can be an incentive for picking up toys. Inviting a friend over can be an incentive for finishing chores. To offer an incentive you might say, "Hey, I have a deal for you—if you can finish that homework in a half hour, you can have 15 extra minutes to play your video game"; or "If you can get this done by 8:00, let's play a game"; or "If you help me out by doing your chore, I'll have time to read to you." Connect through a hug or an "I love you" to help your child trust you have their best interest at heart. Keep expectations achievable, and give them a hand to help them experience success.

A more formal reward system can be created in which stickers or tokens can be earned by accomplishing daily tasks. The tasks may include, for example, getting dressed, brushing teeth, using the bathroom, eating breakfast, and helping with the dishes. Stickers or tokens can be saved up and exchanged for a toy or a special outing. (Read more about tips and mistakes related to the use of incentives in Chapter 9.)

Kids like to know what's happening when. Keep a big family calendar and point out special events that are upcoming so they can be mentally prepared for changes in routine. For many kids with ADHD or autism, reminders about expectations for behavior prior to a situation that is hard for them to manage can also help them be prepared mentally and stay on track during the event. "Be good" is not specific enough! For example, it's helpful to review rules about sharing and taking turns before a playdate, review rules about using good manners before a family gathering, and review rules about staying by the shopping cart before a trip to the store. Role plays can help kids gain skills for special situations. For example, you might role-play the use of table manners before attending a dinner at a fancy restaurant—but avoid being overly serious about it. Your child or teen will be much more receptive if you make it playful and fun. An incentive for following the rules and reminders about the incentive may help them remember what you talked about. If you're in the car, sitting in church, or at a restaurant, offer some fidget toys or a notebook to draw in. Sitting quietly with nothing to do is unrealistic for most kids wired for autism or ADHD.

Kids with brain-based challenges do best with regular routines. Develop routines for getting ready for school, after school, and bedtime. Stay consistent so they develop habits and know what to expect, but also be flexible within your routines. It's okay to change the schedule in favor of a fun outing, to save homework for later so your teen can hang out with friends after school, or let your child stay up a little later now and then to watch a favorite show. Staying attuned, empathic, and playful are much more important than getting every chore done right or getting to bed exactly on time.

Finally, remember to listen. Kids with neurodivergence sometimes have a whole lot to say, and they often have a great sense of humor. It's easy for any of us to get overwhelmed and tune our kids out. When we take the time to listen, laugh, and get interested in their interests, we can build a stronger, more secure connection.

Tip About Schoolwork

High academic achievement is not a healthy goal for families with kids who have brain differences. All kids need downtime and play-time each day. Kids with any form of neurodivergence may have a high energy level and a high need to move and be active or they struggle more. Family time should include plenty of play and fun. As discussed in Chapter 4, it's important to avoid taking respon-sibility for your child's school success. Homework should not be a nightly battle. If your child has deficits that affect learning and schoolwork, it's important for the teacher to observe the problems and find out why your child is struggling. The school may have unrealistic expectations for your child. Advocate for your child's legal right to receive testing and appropriate accommodations.

If you're homeschooling your child, of course you'll be provid-ing the assistance and accommodations, but keep the schoolwork time to school time. After the school day ends, let it all go and find ways to enjoy closeness and connection.

Ten-year-old Norm and his Aunt Louisa:

Norm's aunt had taken guardianship of Norm. He'd experienced early trauma and had ASD and learning disabilities. Every evening Louisa tutored Norm through every piece of homework so that Norm could achieve straight As. The process took an inordinate amount of time. Norm was involved in the special education pro-gram at school, but the school had become dependent upon Lou-isa as a personal tutor. Norm did very little at school, but he always brought his completed work to school the next day because Louisa devoted all her time tediously helping Norm at home. The work did not match Norm's developmental ability because the school didn't fully grasp how he struggled. Norm described himself as "stupid" because Louisa had to walk him through every piece of the schoolwork. He and Louisa were tense and irritable with each other every evening. There was very little fun or playful affection between them.

Norm's therapist encouraged Louisa to tell the school that she was going to stop helping Norm at home so she could focus on building a more secure attachment with Norm and also so his teachers could evaluate Norm's actual performance level. Louisa was shocked at the suggestion initially, but then she talked to the school. Louisa and Norm started to play a game together each night and Norm had more free time to go outside and play with the neighbor kids.

The school began to see what Norm could and couldn't do, and a new, more effective individualized education plan (IEP) was put in place at school. From then on, Norm only brought home assignments that he could finish himself at home. Louisa did help Norm with homework when he asked for help.

PRENATAL ALCOHOL OR DRUG EXPOSURE

Chapter 1 gave a brief overview of brain differences resulting from prenatal substance exposure. Let's delve into this a little more thoroughly, beginning with alcohol exposure, which is the most toxic to the unborn child of all the substances that mothers may ingest. The affected newborn has a less developed brain that is actually smaller in size than the brain of newborn infants who are not affected. Their prefrontal brain may be vastly underdeveloped and lacking the rich network of connections that should be present at birth. This leaves the child with deficits in the brain structures needed to adequately manage their impulses, tolerate frustration, think logically, make plans, solve problems, and anticipate outcomes. Furthermore, the child's corpus callosum, the structure that runs between the right and left hemispheres, is underdeveloped, hampering communication between important regions of the brain. Structures responsible for memory, learning, processing emotions, and motor control are also underdeveloped and underfunctioning.

Fetal alcohol syndrome (FAS) is one of the conditions under the umbrella of FASD, and one of its defining aspects is its physical characteristics, including a lack of groove between the nose and mouth, a thin upper lip, a flat face, smaller eye openings, and an upturned nose, to name just a few. On average, the IQ of children with FAS is lower than the IQ of other kids with FASD. One study (Fadeeva & Nenasteva, 2022) found that the average IQ of individuals with FASD was 79.5 and the average IQ for individuals with FAS was 69.5. (An average IQ is 100.) However, overall, the IQ of affected children and teens can vary widely.

Whether IQ is low or within the normal range, memory functioning is spotty. Kids with FASD may remember something one day and have no memory of it the next. They lack abstract thinking and may be able to parrot things that are told to them or read a page of text while failing to understand the real meaning of the words. The emotional and social functioning of kids with FASD often resembles that of a much younger child, even if they have an average IQ. For example, an older child may have tantrums, interrupt others, talk or laugh too loudly, and tell jokes that only younger children appreciate. They may prefer hanging out with kids younger than they are because their interests are similar. Kids their own age may avoid them or even bully them because of their differences.

Kids with FASD often make up false stories with no awareness that they are lying. This is called *confabulation*. It's innate to FASD and may never disappear. Due to their brain challenges, they may not recognize the difference between what's "mine" and "yours," so they lack appropriate boundaries and take things that aren't theirs. They're often impulsive and unable to think through their actions. They may perseverate on things, which means their brain gets stuck and they repeat the same thought over and over, perhaps related to something they really want or something that makes them anxious.

Although therapy and sensitive parenting may mitigate symptoms related to traumatic stress and attachment difficulties, the core FASD symptoms related to their brain challenges will continue. Brain development continues into their 20s and managing their symptoms may get a little easier with age, but your child will likely continue to struggle with inherent FASD characteristics, such as impulse control, problem solving, critical thinking, and social skills throughout adulthood.

One bright spot in all this is that kids with FASD can have innate strengths and talents that were not removed by the alcohol exposure. Most commonly, they can be musical, artistic, or athletic, and they can have a good sense of humor. Be sure and encourage your child or teen to explore their interests and talents. Involving them in music, art, dance, or sports and showing enthusiasm for their efforts will help them feel better about themselves and feel more secure with you at the same time.

At-Home Accommodations

Living life as a child with brain problems caused by prenatal substance exposure is hard. They feel it when they frustrate or disappoint their parents, siblings, or friends. They suffer when they're left out or rejected by others. They feel badly when they can't remember things or control their impulses. They're frustrated when they don't understand conversations or the meaning behind others' words.

Attuning to your child's limitations and tailoring your expectations to match their capacities academically, socially, emotionally, and behaviorally is critical. If you expect them to function like other kids their age, your child or teen will feel like a disappointment and struggle with poor self-esteem and self-protective defenses. Furthermore, Diane Malbin (2017, p. 33) cautions that kids with FASD have "on and off" days due to inconsistent functioning of their brain. The "on" days, unfortunately, can trick us into believing the child can perform better if they just try harder. The truth is the child has no control over these day-to-day changes in the functioning of their brain.

At-home accommodations for kids with FASD may include hands-on assistance with day-to-day tasks. For example, offer encouragement and assistance with daily routines, such as getting ready in the morning, getting ready for bed, meals, showers, and homework time. Another example of an often-needed accommodation in the home is assistance with toileting issues, especially with younger kids, although older kids also may struggle in this area. The parent might set up a schedule for using the bathroom with reminders and supervision for hand washing and other toileting behaviors. The evening may go better for the whole family when after-dinner chores are accomplished as a team, with everyone working together. Joint efforts create a sense of belonging, safety, and self-worth. Hold on to your mentalizing state. Applying the building blocks for attachment security through attunement, empathy, affection, and playfulness with acceptance and a gentle demeanor will help your child trust that you love them and your intentions are positive.

The use of positive incentives to stay on task can be helpful for some kids along with encouragement and gentle reminders, but incentives aren't useful for all kids with FASD due to their brain's inability to think ahead and foresee the reward that will follow their actions. If your child isn't motivated by rewards, it's simply a symptom of their brain challenges.

Some parents attempt to use negative consequences to help shape their child's behavior. Erica Liu Wollin (2023), psychologist and adoptive mother of a child with FASD, explains that because kids with FASD can't anticipate the effects of their actions, negative consequences take them by surprise each time. They're confused regarding the meaning of the consequences and they're more likely to damage trust than improve their behaviors.

Negotiating expectations, problem solving, and making compromises is a good way to build trust and connection with many traumatized kids. However, Wollin (2023) states that kids with FASD can become dysregulated by too many words or too many options. They have auditory processing and sensory sensitivities that leave them overstimulated and overwhelmed.

To help your child manage the discussion, keep it simple. Step into your mentalizing state and say, "Help me understand. I want to help." Remember that your child struggles to articulate their thoughts and feelings. Listen carefully and then check out what you heard. "I'm hearing that you're hungry and tired and picking up your room feels like too much for you right now." You might offer a simple solution by saying something like "How about we wait until after we've eaten dinner? I can even help you organize your room if you want."

Show empathy and affection and remind your child of the positive reasons behind your request. You might say, "Remember, I'm just doing my mom job." (See "The Jobs of Moms and Dads" section in Chapter 10.) Or you might say, "My job as a mom is important to me, but I hear what you're saying, too. Can we problem solve? How about this . . . " Be careful not to talk too much and stay open to your child's ideas.

If your child loses the sense of trust or connection that you've built, regain trust before you move on. Building greater attachment security will never remove the symptoms of FASD but it will create a sense that you and your child are a team working together instead of enemies in a battle.

Dale's foster mom repairs and attunes following a breach:
Eleven-year-old Dale is in a foster-to-adoption placement. He has symptoms of FASD and has trouble with trust due to neglect in early life:

Mom: Dale, it's time to take your pills.

Dale: I don't want to!

Mom: (*Raising her voice*) You have to! Get over here right now and take these pills! (*Dale runs and hides behind the couch. Mom realizes she needs to make a repair and attune to Dale's feelings. She crouches down near Dale.*) I'm sorry, Dale, I shouldn't have yelled. I just get worried because I love you and I want to help you be healthy and happy. Can you sit by me here on the couch so we can talk? (*Dale nods and comes and leans on her as she puts an arm around him.*) Dale, I trust the doctor, and he thinks the pills will help you feel better. Is there a reason you don't want to take them?

Dale: Sometimes they get stuck in my throat and it doesn't feel good.

Mom: Oh! I didn't know that! I'll call the doctor and find out if it's okay to crush the pills. If not, I can purchase a special kind of cup that helps with taking pills. Can you do your best with it this morning, and then I'll get this figured out? How does that sound?

Keep in mind that the symptoms inherent to the structure and functioning of the FASD brain won't be cured. Parenting a child with FASD requires a lot from parents, and self-care as well as development of a support system are critical. The goal is an improved quality of life for your child, for you, and for the whole family.

If You're the Biological Mother of a Child Impacted by Alcohol or Drugs in Utero

You may be a biological mother who is now in recovery from substance abuse but who used alcohol or drugs during your pregnancy with your child. If you find yourself in this situation, you aren't alone. Alcoholism and other substance use disorders are emotional illnesses that can't be overcome alone. Your recovery is an enormous achievement. Reach out to others within your recovery community for emotional support for grieving and coming to terms with how your illness affected your child. You are not alone. And ask your healthcare provider for a referral to an individual therapist if you don't already have one. Taking care of your own mental health will allow you to stabilize your recovery, heal from any trauma you may have experienced, and provide stability and security for your child.

Other Substances in Utero

There is much research happening in this area and still much to learn. Although alcohol appears to have the most deleterious impact, all substances in utero can cause injury. The brain and body of the developing fetus are fragile and not meant to be infused with toxins of any sort.

Although alcohol exposure is considered the most harmful substance prenatally, exposure to cigarettes can impact growth and cause behavioral and attentional problems. Opiates, cocaine, or methamphetamine exposure can cause atypical behaviors at birth and a lower weight. Marijuana exposure is associated with attentional and problem-solving deficits and hyperactivity. Opiates in utero are associated with hyperactivity and problems with focus and memory. Cocaine exposure leads to similar problems of attention, memory, and behaviors. Social and behavioral problems are associated with amphetamine exposure. Naturally, multiple drugs in utero lead to increased impact on the fetus. Appropriate evaluation and observation can assist parents and teachers with a thorough understanding of the child's brain-based challenges and guide parents in identifying where their child needs assistance and accommodations both at home and at school.

Identifying FASD

Kids with FASD do better when they've been diagnosed early because once FASD is identified, parents have a better understanding for the cause of their child's behaviors. Increased understanding lowers their frustration and they're able to provide their child with the accommodations they need. At the same time, they can let go of pushing for performance in areas where their child lacks capacity.

If your child wasn't born to you, you'll want to talk to your child's caseworker or adoption agency and get as much information as you can to help determine whether there was alcohol or drug exposure in utero. The rates are quite high among foster and adopted children. Many kids removed from situations involving neglect or abuse had biological parents with addictions. Many parents relinquishing babies are struggling because of substance abuse.

In one study, 156 out of 547 kids in foster and adoptive care were found to have a fetal alcohol exposure diagnosis. Eighty percent of those children had not been previously diagnosed by their medical providers (Chasnoff et al., 2015).

FASD Screening

It's not possible to obtain a prenatal history for all kids. There is research currently underway at San Diego State University (Mattson et al., 2023) to help identify markers for FASD when a history or physical features are absent. If you suspect FASD because of your child's symptoms, there's a screening tool called BRAIN-Online that you can fill out (or your child can fill out if they're at least 18 years of age) through FASD United. Go to *fasdunited.org/brain-online*.

You may not be able to get a definitive diagnosis but the screening will help determine whether there are indicators for the diagnosis.

Medication Algorithm for FASD

Finding the right medications is complicated with FASD. Kids with this brain condition sometimes respond differently to some medications than other kids, and they often need a combination that is difficult to identify. The Canada FASD Research Network has identified a medication algorithm called SimpliFASD (*canfasd.ca/algorithm*) to help determine the best medication combination for each individual with FASD. Parents can share the algorithm with their child's medication provider.

What Do I Tell My Child?

Kids with FASD or in utero exposure to other substances benefit from understanding their condition. They already feel different from other kids their own age, which likely has a negative impact on their self-esteem and sense of belonging. Explaining the impact of substances on the brain of unborn babies helps many kids with FASD make sense of their situation. Explain that many mothers don't know that what they're doing will be harmful, some mothers don't know they're pregnant, and some mothers can't stop because they have an addiction. Explain addiction to your child in simple terms, such as "People who get addicted to alcohol feel like they can't live without it. They can't stop using it without special help."

Your child's therapist can help facilitate the discussion. Stay attuned. Answer your child's questions directly and simply. Keep an affectionate demeanor, emphasize the child's strengths, how important they are to the family, and how much they're loved.

If you're the biological mother, you may worry that informing your child about FASD will impact your relationship. Discuss your concerns with your own therapist and let your child's therapist help you manage the discussion with your child.

Canada FASD Research Network offers guidance for talking to your child or teen about FASD. (See https://canfasd.ca/wp -content/uploads/2019/08/How-to-Explain-an-FASD-Diagnosis -to-your-Child.pdf.)

FASD Resources for Parents

The following organizations offer numerous articles and resources regarding FASD for families and for medical and mental health providers:

- Canada FASD Research Network (*canfasd.ca*)
- FASD United (*fasdunited.org*)
- UK National Organisation for FASD (*nationalfasd.org.uk*)
- University of Washington Fetal Alcohol and Drug Unit National Directory of Resources (*fadu.psychiatry.uw.edu/resources*)

Six-year-old Dante and his aunt:
Dante had been exposed to alcohol in utero. Dante's aunt was fostering Dante and planning to adopt if his mother was unable to complete court requirements and stay sober. Dante, age 6, had never had structure or routine. He had meltdowns when his aunt gave him directions of any sort. However, through family ther-

apy, Dante's aunt learned about the ingredients for secure attachment. She often gave Dante *messages of love* and reminded him of the *magical cord of love* they talked about in therapy (see Chapter 4). She developed great skill in managing Dante's behaviors in a way that didn't feel like an assault. For most disruptive behaviors throughout the day, she called Dante over and gave him a little side hug, then spoke softly to him to calm his nervous system. For some tasks, she used incentives to motivate Dante. For example, to help him stay seated at dinner, she whispered in his ear, "Dante, you'll get a little extra dessert if you can stay in your chair." When Dante got fidgety, his aunt gave him a little wink and he calmed himself, remembering the extra dessert. If he began confabulating, his aunt would interrupt him very kindly and say, "Now Dante, this is a good story, but I want you to remember it's a pretend story, okay?" To help him get ready for bed without a fuss, she chatted with him as he showered and brushed his teeth. She knew that Dante functioned better when he felt connected and safe, so she read to him each night and gave him a big bedtime hug. In the morning, she sat with him while they ate breakfast and prepared him for the day's schedule. When she dropped him off at school she reminded him that she'd be sending him hearts and candies through the magical cord of love.

Dante's therapist taught his aunt how to manage the three stages of the meltdown (as described in Chapter 7). Over the 4 months Dante had been with his aunt, his meltdowns had decreased in length and intensity. He had become used to the routine and was easier to manage, but he still needed lots of supervision, teaching, and reminders to get through the tasks of the day.

SENSORY PROBLEMS

Trouble receiving and using information from the senses is a condition called sensory processing disorder (SPD). SPD can be a big problem and can cause many challenging behaviors. Any child can struggle with SPD, but due to underdevelopment of important regions of the brain, children with FASD, ASD, and ADHD are especially at risk. Babies who weren't held due to neglect, orphanage care, or time in neonatal intensive care following premature birth are also at risk because the development of sensory regions in the brain is dependent upon early stimulation of the senses.

Kids with SPD experience sensory input as if the volume button is turned on full blast or the volume button is turned way down. They may vacillate between high and low, as if their nervous system can't decide how to read the sensory input. If the volume is too high, their brain is unable to filter out the input and their nervous system is overloaded. Experiencing normal sights, sounds, smells, and tastes can create a cacophony in their brain. They may become irritable or angry with certain tastes or smells, the textures of certain foods, the feeling of certain fabrics, bright fluorescent lights, the sound of someone repeatedly tapping their feet, or with the feeling of tags in their clothes.

When sensory receptors are turned down, kids have trouble feeling the sensory input and have a need for more. They seek stimulation in any way they can, perhaps through spinning, pushing, jumping, or banging things.

Typically, kids aren't able to articulate what's going on. When parents aren't aware of their child's sensory difficulties, they may assume the child's behaviors are simply meant to drive the parent crazy. Living with sensory problems in a world where people don't understand what's going on with you can lead to feeling like an outsider. Living with constant nervous system activation can cause anxiety, depression, social problems, and learning problems.

An evaluation with an occupational therapist can help identify the sensory problems and occupational therapy can help improve sensory functioning. Retraining the brain to process sensory input takes time, however. It is important to attune to stimulation that is difficult for your child and to find stimulation that is helpful. There are many sensory toys available on the market that help with symptoms of SPD, such as fidget toys for squeezing and manipulating, wobble boards, balance boards, and swings that provide focused sensations for help with organizing the nervous system. You may be able to remove some unnecessary sensory triggers at home simply by removing clutter, turning the volume down on music and television, purchasing unscented detergents and lotions, and removing tags from your child's clothing. Work with your child's occupational therapist regarding what else you can do to support your child at home.

TAKING CARE OF "YOU"

There's nothing more meaningful than giving a child who's been through hard times the love and connection they need. However, whether you're an adoptive or biological parent raising a child with brain differences, it's an extremely stressful role due to the intensity of your child's needs, the long-term nature of their needs, and the lack of understanding from the community and maybe even from extended family members (Wollin, 2023). I strongly believe the best thing you can do for yourself is participate in your own therapy and become a part of a community of parents facing challenges with their kids by joining a support group. Couple therapy can also help couples stay strong in the face of caregiving demands. Chapter 11 provides you with more ideas for taking care of yourself and creating the support system you need to help fill your own bucket throughout this very important journey.

PERFECT IS THE ENEMY OF THE GOOD

This was first said by the famous French writer and activist, Voltaire. He had it right. The belief that we need to be perfect can lead to self-judgments and immobilize us with fear. Furthermore, when we set out to prove to ourselves or others that we're perfect parents, we focus on all the wrong things. We think too much about the opinions of others. We fail to attune to the internal state of our child or ourselves. We focus on achievements instead of connection. We have unreasonable expectations that cause our kids to feel inadequate. We're inflexible about rules and tasks instead of making room for feelings and needs. We're frightened by our child's uniqueness or by any nonconformity to society's standards because we're focused on the judgments of others.

Kids with brain differences caused by neurodivergence, in utero substance exposure, or early trauma may or may not be good with academics. They may not exhibit social graces or have lofty aspirations. But they have fascinating interests, talents, and unique thoughts and ideas. When we let go of perfectionistic tendencies and step into a mentalizing state of being, we're able to be fully present with our kids, flexible, and accepting of mess-ups and messiness. We can celebrate and enjoy their differences in a family where no one has to earn their way into acceptance and love.

I invite you to join the ranks of other parents who let go of living up to perfectionistic standards for themselves or for their children in exchange for more laughter, more play, and more fun!

Chapter 7

Managing the Three Stages of a Meltdown

MELTDOWNS DESERVE A CHAPTER OF THEIR OWN because they're such a common symptom for kids impacted by attachment trauma and so incredibly challenging for parents to manage. Children and teens can have meltdowns that last for hours. They may scream names and obscenities, hit, kick, throw things, punch holes in walls, and even try to bite. These behaviors can certainly be shocking, and parents may feel hurt, angry, anxious, fearful, sad, and hopeless. The parent may think, "I'm a failure" and "My child is bad." Parents may react with angry attempts to control their child or push the child away. If this has been your child or teen, you may live in fear of these episodes.

TWO TYPES OF MELTDOWNS

Meltdowns are no fun—they are no fun for parents, siblings, or other family members and definitely no fun for the child experiencing meltdowns. Neuroscientist Dan Siegel and parenting expert Tina Bryson (2011) describe two types of meltdowns: "downstairs" and "upstairs." Upstairs meltdowns are what parents traditionally call tantrums. The child wants something and is consciously going after what they want. In a downstairs meltdown, the child has completely lost all control.

Both tantrums and downstairs meltdowns are to be expected at times with children age 5 and younger. Almost every parent has experienced the embarrassment of a screaming toddler in the candy aisle of the grocery store. However, young children with a history of attachment trauma may have multiple upstairs brain tantrums per day as well as downstairs brain meltdowns that last for hours. Furthermore, tantrums and downstairs meltdowns continue for many traumatized kids all the way into adolescence for the reasons outlined in Chapter 1. The likelihood of ongoing meltdowns increases for traumatized kids who have additional brain challenges caused by prenatal substance exposure, neurodivergence, or an inherited mental health condition.

UPSTAIRS BRAIN TANTRUMS

If your child is having an upstairs tantrum, they're frustrated and overwhelmed with not getting the thing they want in the moment, but they're still present enough that they can stop the tantrum behavior if something else catches their interest or when it becomes certain they're not going to achieve the thing they desire. It's imperative not to provide reinforcement by giving in to demands during the tantrum. Hold a firm boundary about their request but modulate your voice and keep your eyebrows slightly elevated, not furrowed. Keep breathing and remind yourself that it's not personal. Avoid negotiating, pleading, or bribing. If you lose your mentalizing state and become angry, it will likely trigger their stored trauma and a full-fledged downstairs meltdown.

If your child is choosing to tantrum in the check-out aisle to get candy, for example, stay calm, stay close, and say something like "I'm doing my mom job because I care about you and candy's not healthy. The answer's going to remain no." It's also helpful to show that you do understand how hard it is for your child—and it truly is. You might say, "I'm sorry, I know it's hard to be a kid sometimes."

Continue riding out the tantrum until your child calms down. Continue to breathe and remind yourself that most people at the store understand and if they don't, it's of no consequence to you. If you're in that check-out aisle, you might wish to ask the clerk to watch your cart while you take the child to the car and sit a bit with them while they calm down. If you're at home, avoid sending the child to their room. Instead, stay calm and nearby until they calm down.

THE DOWNSTAIRS MELTDOWN

The downstairs meltdown is driven by the lower regions of the brain—a brain that is "firing" due to some type of trigger. For kids with a history of attachment trauma, the downstairs meltdown can come on swiftly and aggressively. This type of quick change in affect state is commonly brought on by a trigger that activated feelings and perceptions connected to early trauma stored within their memory networks. The downstairs meltdown takes on a life of its own, in a sense. Your child is no more in control of it than you are.

The trigger may not be obvious or may seem incredibly minor to you. Remember, it happens immediately and subconsciously and the child or teen isn't in control of it when it happens. The trigger might simply be an expression on your face or a voice tone that triggered early feelings of insignificance, powerlessness, hurt, or fear. When early trauma is triggered, feelings and perceptions connected to the younger child part of them are activated. In a sense, they're operating with a primitive young child part of their brain. In this state, the child or teen has no access to logic or reason. The prefrontal brain is shut down, and the very primitive downstairs brain is in charge.

The Three Phases of the Downstairs Meltdown

Our colleague, Ann Potter (2011a), developed a way of understanding the progression of a typical downstairs meltdown along with management strategies that parents find to be extremely helpful. The theory identifies three specific phases of a meltdown:

- Phase 1: Acting out (panic)
- Phase 2: Acting in (shame)
- Phase 3: Repair and reconnection (emotional pain)

Each phase has distinct characteristics and specific parent management tools. Meltdowns can be reviewed and dissected in therapy. Your therapist can help you identify the different phases and coach you on how to handle your child specifically. Let's take a closer look at a meltdown in order to gain a better understanding of the different phases.

Flora came into a family therapy session and described her granddaughter's meltdown as follows:

> My 8-year-old granddaughter, Leah, had come home from school in an angry mood. Every attempt to interact with her had been met with an angry retort of some sort, and I found myself growing increasingly weary and frustrated. Through dinner she continued to be grumpy, whiny, and difficult. My husband and I invited her to sit between us and watch a children's show after dinner, but the behaviors continued.
>
> I decided that she was just overtired and needed sleep. I invited her to put on her pajamas for bed, and then the giant meltdown started. Objects in her bedroom began flying through the air, and her body turned into what looked like a flopping fish on the bed. My granddaughter was pulling all the bedclothes off the bed as she was rolling around and screaming, "Go away! Get out of here! I don't want you here!" My instinct was to get angry but because I understand more than I ever did before about meltdowns, I took a deep breath, sat down on the floor, and said, "Wow, I wish I understood what you're feeling." I stayed very quiet while she rolled and shouted for a little while longer, and then she suddenly reached out for me as she began sobbing uncontrollably. I got up next to her and took her in my arms and held her. I rocked her side to side on the bed as she continued to sob. My heart broke for her when she cried, "It's not fair! All the other kids live with a mom and dad. Their parents are married, and they are young, and they have a house and brothers and sisters and they do fun stuff as a family. My parents were never even married. I hate going to my dad's house; I don't even like all those kids over there, and I feel uncomfortable. I don't even get to see my mom that often. I don't have brothers or sisters here to play with, and I just feel so, so sad."

I continued to hold her and rock her and I said, "I'm so glad you could tell me," and I said, "I'm so sorry," over and over, until she calmed down, like you've taught me to do in the family therapy sessions. Then my husband came in, and we took turns holding her and telling her how much we love her. She gave us big hugs and told us she loved us, and then settled right down and went to sleep. The evening could have ended in anger but because I was able to attune to all that grief and sadness beneath her big meltdown, it became an opportunity to help her with her grief and make her feel more secure with us.

Phase 1: Acting Out—Panic

Phase 1 of a meltdown is a child's version of a panic attack. At this stage, your child's brain is stuck. The emotional limbic area of the brain has been activated and the prefrontal thinking part of the brain is not functioning. Your child is in a state in which they can't tell the difference between the present and the past. They may be experiencing an emotional flashback: a recurrence of intense emotion associated with a past trauma. They have no access to the rational, thinking region of the brain and they're not fully present in their body. This disconnection from themselves is a form of dissociation. They're in full-on fight–flight and verbally and/or physically out of control. In this stage, touch is typically not tolerated. This stage can last anywhere from a couple of minutes to several hours.

In the example above, Leah was clearly having a difficult time upon her arrival from school. Flora didn't know it, but Leah had been triggered by overhearing other kids talk about their families. Flora attempted to help Leah calm herself, but nothing seemed to be working. Flora fed her and tried to help Leah relax, but to no avail. They were headed into Phase 1 of the meltdown, no matter what. Phase 1, in this example, is identified by the complete loss of control of Leah's emotions and actions. Her prefrontal cortex had shut down, and there was really no way that Flora could have "talked" or "threatened" Leah out of Phase 1.

Managing Phase 1

Handling Phase 1 requires some very specific strategies. In this phase, your child requires some physical space around them. You may be able to invite them to their room or another part of the house where they can safely have some physical space while you stay nearby. They may scream at you to leave but it's best to stay, perhaps just outside the door to the room where they can see you. Don't shut the door or block the door. On the other hand, if you attempt to close in on your child, they may react like a cornered animal. Once your child is in a full-blown meltdown, isolating them or threatening punishments will trigger a stronger fight-or-flight response and lengthen the episode.

Throughout Phase 1 of the meltdown, say to your child, "I'm here, I love you. You're having some big feelings. I'll give you some space to cool down but I won't go away. I'll be right here."

Remind yourself to breathe and tell yourself, "I'm okay, we'll get through this" and "I can use my calm nervous system to calm my child's nervous system." Your calm voice and presence will help ground your child and shorten the length of the meltdown.

If you have a partner, make a plan to tag team so that one stays nearby while the other takes a break. This will help you manage your own energy level and keep you both calm.

Once Flora realized that Leah was in Phase 1, she sat close, calmed her own voice, and just attuned to Leah. Flora did not try to stop Leah from throwing things or screaming. If she had, the meltdown would have escalated. Flora also stayed close but gave Leah space at the same time. Leah was screaming, "Get out of here!" but she didn't really mean it. Flora gave her enough space without leaving.

Phase 2: Acting In—Shame

In Phase 2, your child's brain is still stuck. The prefrontal cortex is still not engaged. At this stage, your child may be embarrassed and flooded with shame by what has just happened. Although your child won't articulate it, they are flooded by negative thoughts, such as "I'm a bad kid" or "No one loves me" or "No one can handle me." The child in Phase 2 is beginning to come back into their body, back to the present, and may be sobbing in despair or withdrawing and shutting down. If you move closer, they may continue to push you away, yelling, "Leave me alone!" or "Don't ever talk to me again!" or "I hate you!" In the next breath, they may yell, "Don't go . . . don't leave me." You may feel both pushed and pulled. Your child doesn't want to believe they need you because that feels too vulnerable, but they do need you at the same time. Early life feelings of rejection or abandonment are strongly activated.

It's very difficult to discern when a child has left Phase 1 and is in Phase 2. It may gradually become clearer as you begin to deal with meltdowns using this method and you notice their particular signs and signals that they're entering each phase. Your therapist will help you dissect your child's meltdowns and gain insight into what's happening in the different stages.

Managing Phase 2

Managing Phase 2 is similar to managing Phase 1. Continue to provide the appropriate amount of space, but as your child moves through the phases, you'll probably be able to move the boundary closer. If your child is in their room, you may be able to sit on the bed instead of standing in the hallway.

Nurturing messages of love and safety are necessary. Because they're becoming more grounded in the present, your child is experiencing intense shame. Continue to help ground your child to the present moment. You might ask questions such as "Can you feel your feet on the ground?" or "We're in your room—can you notice the color of the walls?" until your child is oriented. At this stage, there's very little real conversation. The logical thinking brain is still not fully operational. Your child may be able to tolerate some touch, but perhaps not. Attune to your child to find what's helpful.

In the meltdown example between Leah and her grandmother, Leah moved to Phase 2 once she started to talk and explain why she was so upset. Flora let Leah say what she needed to say. Flora didn't interrupt or try to correct Leah's thoughts or beliefs. If she had, Leah probably would have moved back into Phase 1.

Phase 3: Repair and Reconnection—Emotional Pain

Once you cross into Phase 3, you know that your child's brain is finally unstuck. The prefrontal cortex is engaged again, and your child is fully back in the present. In this stage, your child is still feeling ashamed and likely fearful of rejection. Your child still feels disconnected and all alone. Having a meltdown is more traumatic than witnessing one. Your child needs to connect with you physically and emotionally in order to fully recover.

Managing Phase 3

During Phase 3, it's time to draw your child close and reassure them that you're glad they're back and feeling better. Now is the time to repair the disconnect through the building blocks of attunement, empathic responses, and affection. It's still not time to talk through things or talk about what they could have said or done. Just focus on the reconnection and stay positive. You can say, "I love you, you're okay now. Can I sit with you? Can I give you a hug?"

Don't worry that connecting now will reward them for the meltdown. It won't feel like a reward to your child. It will feel like a lifeline.

In Leah's meltdown, once Leah allowed Flora to hold her, Flora knew that Leah was present and thinking again. Grandma did a wonderful job of listening and attuning to Leah's sad feelings about being different from other kids and missing her birth mother. The hugs and expression of love composed the repair work done after this meltdown. Grandma and Grandpa did not lecture or scold Leah for having a fit, screaming, and throwing stuff around. There was no need to punish any of Leah's behaviors. They knew Leah had been triggered and had been unable to control her body or her brain. Her grandparents did a wonderful job of managing this meltdown. Over time, they hope that Leah will learn to express her feelings and thoughts without being so overwhelmed by them.

Suzie's mother manages her meltdown:

Suzie, age 11, spent 2 years in foster care when her mother was struggling to recover from a drug addiction. Now fully in recovery, Suzie's mother is learning strategies to improve the connection and calm Suzie's brain but Suzie still has occasional meltdowns. On this occasion, Suzie had spent the night with a friend and had come home exhausted, so her brain was taxed. She asked her mother for a popsicle, and her mother replied, "I'm fixing lunch right now, and you can have a popsicle for dessert." Suzie's brain, in her exhausted state, could not manage the "waiting feeling," and she fell into Phase 1 of a meltdown. Suzie fell on the floor and began writhing and kicking, while wailing loudly. Suzie's mom reminded herself, "This is Suzie's trauma brain. She's getting better but she's overtired. I can handle this."

Mom: I'm giving you some space, Suzie, but I'm right here. As soon as your brain calms down, we'll snuggle and talk. (*Suzie continues the meltdown at full throttle on the kitchen floor for about 10 minutes, while her mom waits quietly off to the side.*)

Mom: Remember, Suzie, you're here in the kitchen, and I'm here nearby. I love you. When you're calm, we will snuggle and talk.

Suzie: (*Curls into a fetal position; begins sobbing*) [Beginning Phase 2 of the meltdown]

Mom: I'm still here, Suzie. I'm coming into the kitchen, okay? I love you.

Suzie: Go away! (*Continues to sob*) No, don't leave! (*Calms down and reaches for her mother*)

Mom: (*Moves in and holds Suzie, rocking her back and forth*) I love you, I'm glad you're letting me hold you. How about we eat lunch and then have a popsicle together?

KEEP THE FAITH!

Meltdowns are exhausting and scary. Staying with the strategies in this chapter may require a real leap of faith. Use your support system! Do the very best you can to stay in a mentalizing state and implement the strategies for all three phases of the meltdown. Attachment security will build over time, and the meltdowns will be gradually lessened.

Chapter 8

Interrupting the Falling Dominoes

Do you remember setting up a string of dominoes as a child and then watching them rapidly fall, one after the other? Psychologist Ann Potter (2011b) has termed the chain of events leading up to a meltdown, arguing, or other acting-out behaviors as "dominoes." In situations with your child, a string of dominoes can fall very rapidly.

IDENTIFYING YOUR CHILD'S DOMINOES

Reflecting upon the typical cascade of dominoes in your home can help you intervene and interrupt stuck patterns.

Your Child's Vulnerability Factors

Certain situations narrow your child's window of tolerance for distress.

Check the factors you believe increase your child's vulnerability to become triggered:

- ☐ Fatigue
- ☐ Hunger
- ☐ Illness
- ☐ When Mom or Dad is stressed
- ☐ Recent consequences for misbehavior
- ☐ Schoolwork stress
- ☐ Problems with friends
- ☐ Other: _____

Dad attunes to Andy's fatigue:

Andy celebrated his 17th birthday on Saturday. His parents were amazed that he managed his behavior throughout the entire day. He kept himself relatively calm, he used good manners, he ate a reasonable amount of cake, and he thanked everyone for his gifts. On Sunday morning Andy woke up very crabby and was headed toward a meltdown by noon because his brother ate a piece of his cake without asking. Andy was vulnerable to a meltdown because he was mentally exhausted after keeping himself in check all day on his birthday. Instead of taking away his new presents when he got mad about the cake, Andy's dad took some time to sit with and connect with him. Andy's dad validated how hard Andy had worked to keep himself under control the day before, and how tired he must feel. He validated Andy's sad feelings about the cake and helped him get back on track by becoming mindful of his tired feelings.

Your Child's Triggers

Think about inciting situations that start the dominoes falling. Look back at the triggers you checked for your child in Chapter 2. Circle the triggers you might be able to reduce or remove by use of a more attuned approach.

Even with attunement, many triggers will be unavoidable. When your child or teen is calm and receptive, bring up the topic of triggers. Explain that triggers are situations that cause us to have sudden big feelings. Share your own triggering situations, including situations that have nothing to do with them. If your child is receptive, brainstorm some of their triggers and your own triggers. By mentalizing together in a nonjudgmental manner, your child's awareness will grow.

Your Child's Negative Beliefs

As described in Chapter 2, the child or teen with a history of attachment trauma has developed many negative beliefs about self, others, and the world, and their most negative beliefs will come to the forefront when they're triggered.

Look back at the negative beliefs you identified for your child in Chapter 2. Think about how you might counter these negative beliefs through positive, affectionate messages. List some positive messages you would like your child to hear:

_____

_____

_____

_____

_____

Your Child's Emotions

Big emotions are part of the chain of toppling dominoes. An emotion can be triggered automatically. One emotion can be a trigger to more emotions, negative thoughts, or body sensations, and emotions can definitely lead to big behaviors.

Check the emotions your child struggles to tolerate:

- ☐ Shame and guilt
- ☐ Anxiety
- ☐ Anger
- ☐ Frustration
- ☐ Powerlessness
- ☐ Hurt
- ☐ Grief
- ☐ Sadness

Remember that when kids experience intense emotions, they often think they'll never feel better. When the timing is right, remind your child that feelings come and feelings go, and that all feelings are normal.

Your Child's Sensations

Body sensations can be part of the chain of toppling dominoes. Kids with a history of attachment trauma are often cut off from their body sensations, yet driven by them. Many kids interpret their body sensations as illness. We can all relate to uncomfortable sensations that accompany intense emotions, including tension in the neck, back, or chest, a headache, or nausea.

Body sensations are signals to the brain that something is up. If your child or teen complains of a headache or stomachache, be aware there may be underlying emotions. Take the opportunity to listen, attune, and co-regulate.

Six-year-old Sasha and her mom:

Mom noticed that when Sasha was tired, she was easily angered and had little patience for her siblings. The following vignette illustrates how Sasha's mom helps her become more aware of her body sensations:

Mom: (*Listening to Sasha, who's outside on the swing set, yelling and bossing her siblings around*) Sasha, can you come in the house for a minute? I want to talk with you.

Sasha: What, Mom? I'm playing—I don't want to come inside. I'm not doing anything wrong. They're not playing the game right.

Mom: I'm sure that's true. Sometimes your brother and sister want to play their way, don't they, and that upsets you. It's hard to be the big sister. I have another question for you, though. I'm wondering if your brain and your body are telling you that you're tired, and the tired feelings are coming out in your words. Do you think that could be true?

Sasha: I'm not tired. They're just being mean.

Mom: Hmm, I'm wondering if your brain and body worked so hard this week doing all that great schoolwork that they just need to rest a bit. Let's sit down on the couch together for a little while and see if that's what's going on inside. (*Sasha stomps over to the couch and sits down. After a minute, she has a big yawn.*) That was a nice yawn. I wonder if your body says, "Hey Sasha, let me rest. I'm tired."

Sasha: My feet are tired.

Mom: Yes, I bet they are. Maybe we should let them rest here on the couch. What about your brain? Is it tired?

Sasha: I don't know.

Mom: Sasha, it's okay to take a break and rest. I think your body and brain would play so much better with your brother and sister if you just took a rest. I'll stay with you on the couch, and we can rest together.

Sasha: (*Falls asleep for about half an hour and wakes up*) Mom, you were right, my brain was tired. I think it's better now. Can I go back out and play?

Mom: Yes, you sure can.

If Mom had made Sasha come in and take a nap, a meltdown probably would have occurred. Mom is trying to help Sasha become more in touch with her body so that she can learn to read her own signs.

The Final Domino: The Meltdown or Acting-Out Behavior

The meltdown or other actingout behavior becomes the final domino toppling over. When you begin thinking in terms of dominoes, you'll learn to start thinking backward from the big behaviors to the dominoes that preceded the crisis. This will give you important information that may help you remove some of the dominoes and change course when they're headed for a crisis. After a crisis, when both of you are calm, you may be able to sit down and calmly examine the dominoes that led up to the storm together. This nonjudgmental, logical approach to examining the chain of events activates your child's logical thinking brain, minimizes the shame and emotional reactivity, and encourages problem solving to prevent the dominoes from falling next time.

Interrupting the Dominoes

Attuning to your child's activated nervous system and providing reassurance and affection can stop the cascade of falling dominoes and bring them back into their window of tolerance. Sofia's mom provided attunement, affection, and reassurance and asked Sofia to reassure the little Sofia in her heart. She stopped the cascade of falling dominoes.

Sofia's mom calms Sofia's activated nervous system and interrupts the falling dominoes:

Sofia, age 8, has come home from school in an activated state:

> **Sofia:** Mom! Come here right now. I need you. I need you right now!
>
> **Mom:** (*Entering the room*) I didn't hear you come in the door. (*Attuning and connection*) It sounds like you're kind of upset. Come sit with me on the couch for a minute.
>
> **Sofia:** I'm starving. I need a snack right now! I can't wait!
>
> **Mom:** (*Gently putting an arm around her and walking her toward the kitchen*) You know, I'll never let you go hungry. Can you remind the "littler Sofia" who lives inside your heart that everything is okay while I fix you some graham crackers and peanut butter?
>
> **Sofia:** (*Calm now*) Yes, that would be good. I had a bad time on the way home from school. Some boys were calling me names.
>
> **Mom:** I thought maybe something was bothering you. Remember that you can always come to me if you're feeling unsafe.

Erika's dad interrupts the falling dominoes:

Erika, age 10, has a developmental delay in addition to a history of attachment trauma. Dad notices that Erika seems agitated as the family is preparing to leave for church on Wednesday evening. Last Wednesday evening, they didn't make it to church because Erika had a full-blown meltdown:

> **Dad:** Come here, Erika. Let's snuggle on the couch for a few minutes. I love you. Tell me how you're doing.
>
> **Erika:** I don't know. I'm kind of mad.
>
> **Dad:** How come? What are you feeling?
>
> **Erika:** Nobody pays attention to me. Everybody's busy. My friend Mary says she isn't my friend anymore.
>
> **Dad:** Wednesday evenings are busy, aren't they? I can understand that you feel like you don't get enough time with me or with Mom, and I had no idea you were having problems with your friend at school. Tell me more about it . . .

By spending just a little time attuning and responding with sensitivity and affectionate touch, Dad calmed Erika's nervous system and warded off the pending meltdown.

INTERRUPTING YOUR OWN DOMINOES

We're all subject to the human experience of cascading negative emotions, thoughts, and feelings, and our own falling dominoes can easily merge with our child's dominoes.

Figure 8.1 illustrates how the child's falling dominoes cause the parent's dominoes to fall, and how the parent's dominoes in turn cause the child's dominoes to continue to fall. The situation quickly cascades out of control. Awareness of your own dominoes can give you the power to interrupt the patterns in your home.

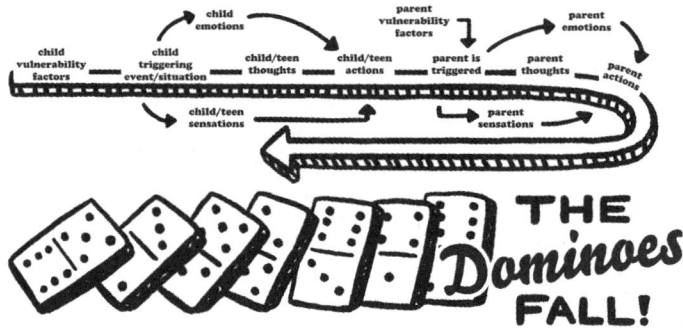

FIGURE 8.1 The child and parent dominoes intersect. *Drawing by Julia Deese.*

Your Vulnerability Factors

When everything piles on you all at once and you don't feel well or your support network is unavailable, do you lose your coping skills?

List the situations that leave you most vulnerable to triggers:

_____

_____

_____

_____

_____

_____

Your Triggers

For many parents, behaviors that are viewed as signs of "disrespect" are most triggering. These challenging behaviors may include talking back, refusing to obey, lying, stealing, and any other acting-out behaviors. Many parents are most triggered by behaviors that embarrass them in public places, in school, or in the family's place of worship. Other parents are most reactive to dangerous or risky behaviors or by actions that are hurtful toward other kids in the family. Some parents are most challenged by behaviors that are "gross," including inappropriate toileting behaviors or poor hygiene.

Identify the behaviors that trigger you the most:

_____

_____

_____

_____

_____

_____

Your Thoughts

Difficult behaviors of children and teens naturally trigger hopeless, anxious, or angry thoughts in their parents. Negative thoughts can be dominoes that lead to emotional reactions.

Judgmental Thoughts

Common judgmental thoughts are "I'm bad" and "My child is bad." Neither is true. Your actions are sometimes driven by fear and anxiety, as your child's actions are. Remind yourself, "My child and I are both vigilant and anxious."

Embarrassed Thoughts

It's natural to feel embarrassed by your child's behaviors. Most people hate to be judged, and our identity is wrapped up in how we're doing as a parent. Critical comments or "looks" from other parents, teachers or school staff, friends, or extended family can be hurtful. Negative thoughts may include "This is humiliating" and "Others are judging me."

Remind yourself, "Others' thoughts are of no consequence to me" and "Besides, they may have more empathy for me than I know."

Hopeless Thoughts

Hopeless thoughts are normal when stress is high. It's hard to see in that moment that there is a bigger meaning to the challenges you face. Negative thoughts may include "Here we go again—this will never get better" and "I might as well give up."

You're choosing a more meaningful life by focusing on the important task of helping your child. Expect your child to move two steps forward and one step back, and then celebrate each small step forward. Remind yourself, "With the help of the therapists, over time, I can help change the course of my child's life."

Anger-Driven Thoughts

Reflect on any negative thoughts that come to you when you're angry. For example, your thoughts may include "My child needs to learn a lesson" and "My child is a spoiled brat."

The truth is that your child or teen is wired to mistrust and self-protect and has brain differences caused by early trauma. Remind yourself, "My child feels unsafe in the world and needs my help to trust and connect."

Negative Thoughts About Your Child's Motivations

The emotional part of your brain may assume your child is intentionally out to hurt you, even when the logical part of your brain knows their behaviors are driven by the brain's response to trauma. Your emotion-driven thoughts may include "My child is disrespecting me" and "My child is out to get me/hurt me."

Remind yourself of the rational, more helpful thought, "My child learned to fear closeness and vulnerability, but deep down my child wants to be close."

Write down any negative thoughts from above that resonate for you or thoughts you don't see listed that trouble you:

_____

_____

_____

_____

_____

_____

Make a list of helpful, rational thoughts here and then put them into your phone so they're handy:

_____

_____

_____

_____

_____

_____

Your Emotions and Sensations

Common emotions carried by parents of children with attachment or trauma issues include shame and guilt, anxiety, anger, frustration, powerlessness, hurt, and grief. These powerful emotions can be immediate and overwhelming.

List the emotions you most struggle with here:

_____

_____

_____

_____

_____

_____

Where do your emotions tend to land in your body?

☐ Tightness in your chest, neck, or shoulders?
☐ Tension in your arms or hands?
☐ Racing heart?
☐ Other: _____

If you can pay attention to your body, you'll know when you need to take a pause, breathe, and use some self-talk.

Your Actions

The next time your child acts out in some way, ask yourself:

- Is my voice loud or harsh?
- Is my facial expression angry?
- Am I using angry words?
- Am I shaming or threatening?

If you can catch yourself, take a pause. Breathe. Drop your shoulders, lower your voice, soften your face, and reassure your child that the two of you can figure this out.

Fifteen-year-old Ted and his mom debrief a situation:

Ted had missed out on dinner with the family. He had complained about the spaghetti and his mom had told him he could go to his room if he didn't like it. He had stormed off to his bedroom and stayed there for the rest of the evening. Before bed, his mom asked if she could come in so they could talk:

Mom: Was it a hard day at school today?

Ted: I had a headache all day. Algebra is stressing me out. I keep forgetting to bring my book home, and now I'm behind.

Mom: I can understand that must be stressful.

Ted: And the food was disgusting at school today. I couldn't even eat it.

Mom: You must have been really hungry. And then you had to go to football practice after school.

Ted: Yeah, the coach really worked us, and it was hot.

Mom: That must have been hard.

Ted: My coach yelled at me. I forgot the play. I felt like an idiot.

Mom: I'll bet you were still beating yourself up about football and algebra when you got home.

Ted: Yeah.

Mom: I wish I had known what a hard day you had. I'm sorry I reacted so strongly to the spaghetti comment. It just hurt my feelings, and I had a stressful day, too. From now on, let's both try to communicate better when you come home, okay?

Ted: Okay.

Mom: Why don't you come to the kitchen and get yourself something to eat?

Ted: Okay. And then do you think you could help me figure out this algebra assignment?

Mom: Sure.

Zak and his mom—cascading dominoes:

In this example, Zak's mom is completely unaware that her dominoes are intersecting with Zak's dominoes. As Zak's actions get triggered, he in turn triggers his mom, and the situation rapidly escalates out of control. Because the cycle reinforces negative thoughts and feelings in both of them, a recurrence is likely.

Nine-year-old Zak enters the house after school, like many children, tired from the day and famished. His mom, still annoyed that Zak left his bed unmade that morning, tells Zak to make his bed and get his homework started. He becomes overwhelmed and throws his book bag. His mom moves into fight-or-flight mode and raises her voice. Zak feels attacked and kicks his book bag. His mom feels like a failure. She shuts down and retreats to her bedroom. Zak escalates into a full-fledged downstairs meltdown and winds up knocking over a lamp when he throws a pillow. Activated by the noise of the breaking lamp, his mom comes out of her bedroom and drags Zak into his room and leaves him there alone. Zak shouts with frustration and then sobs in despair. They both end up feeling rejected, ashamed, and angry.

This scenario may have left you with a headache, but it may help you understand how the parent's dominoes can topple the child's dominoes and vice versa.

Let's sort it all out. First, what factors made Zak's mom more vulnerable to getting triggered?

1. Zak's mom was tired from working all day.
2. She was annoyed that Zak hadn't made his bed that morning.

What were Zak's vulnerability factors?

1. Zak was tired.
2. He was hungry.

We can also assume that if Zak has a history of attachment trauma, he's sensitive to feelings of rejection, has difficulty trusting that adults are on his side, and is easily stressed by school and homework.

Mom and Zak develop a plan:

That evening, when they're both calm, Mom asks Zak to help her come up with a plan so they both can do better next time. She and Zak agree on a plan to have a snack together every day after school and reconnect. This will be a time that Zak can share anything he wants to about his day. They make an agreement that he will try to do homework on his own but will ask her for some help if it's too hard. Mom says she'll make a point to listen and help the best she can and email the teacher if she thinks Zak needs extra help at school. By attuning and developing a plan that is sensitive to Zak's needs, Mom is helping him with trust and connection.

STRENGTHENING CONNECTION AFTER A CRISIS

Taking the time to be emotionally and physically present with your child following any type of acting out will strengthen your child's ability to operate out of their logical brain as they move forward. Any time you are able to reach out to your child when they are feeling bad and pull them closer is an opportunity for forging your relationship and strengthening your child's brain. You might find that during this reconnection phase, you and your child are able to talk at a deeper level about the things that are bothering them. Through these connecting experiences, over time, your child will become more securely attached, which will calm the nervous system, widen the window of tolerance, and increase your child's capacity for problem-focused coping.

Chapter 9

Strategies for Addressing Alarming Behaviors

WHEN KIDS HAVE A STORE OF TRAUMA MEMORIES they are constantly triggered by innocuous events of everyday life along with a sense that there's no one to whom they can turn. Their triggers move them quickly outside of their window of tolerance into the fight-or-flight zone or shutdown zone. Their upstairs brain shuts down and they're driven by the raw feelings firing in their downstairs brain. In this downstairs brain functioning, they lose access to their most mature state. They can't access logical thinking because their upstairs brain has been hijacked. As they function with the thoughts and feelings of their younger self, they're in a primitive survival mode.

Complicating this situation is the fact that for kids with a traumatic history, their most mature state is not nearly as mature as it would be if their early life had been easy. For most kids with a difficult history, the mature state is underdeveloped due to the impact of trauma on their prefrontal brain. The dilemma for us as parents is how to help our kids step into their most mature state, improve their mature state functioning, and settle the traumatized younger part at the same time.

Although closeness with you is key to your child's emotional growth, it's hard to maintain connection during alarming behaviors. Let's look at the behaviors and what you can do.

LYING FOR SELF-PROTECTION

Most kids will tell a lie now and then to get out of trouble. However, if your child had experienced attachment security in their early years, being in trouble with you or their teachers would feel unpleasant but not dangerous. Your child would know deep down that they're loved no matter what and that the upset with you would be temporary. These feelings of security would minimize the lying behavior.

If your child carries stored memories of attachment injuries, disapproval from you or their teachers feels downright dangerous. Fear and insecurity stored in their memory networks automatically send your child into survival mode. They're driven to protect themselves.

What Can I Do?

Let's first get clear about the goal. The road to improving your child's capacity to think and reason and make good decisions is building a secure connection. Yelling or punishments have absolutely no impact on those things but only reinforce feelings of threat, downstairs brain functioning, and the younger child state. Whether their nervous system is in the fight-or-flight zone or the shutdown zone, your child absolutely needs to feel safe with you to access their most mature prefrontal brain functioning. Emotional attunement is required to provide a safe connection.

When your child has told a lie, take a pause and step into the mentalizing state by reminding yourself, "My child is outside the window of tolerance and operating from a younger state. My child needs connection, attunement, and safety to get out of survival mode and back into more mature functioning."

To create a safe connection, avoid using words that are confrontational and judgmental. It's often helpful to use the words "I notice" in a factual, nonjudgmental manner. For example, you might say, "I notice it's hard for you to be accurate with your words when . . . " Attune to the anxiety driving your child's lying behav-

117

ior and respond to the anxiety with reassurance and problem solving. Show appreciation if the child corrects their lie. If the child doesn't correct what you believe is a lie, you can simply say, "I'm trying to believe you, but I'm having a hard time" and then let it go.

Kids with FASD or ASD often are overwhelmed by too much discussion. If your child can tolerate a brief discussion, you might be able to invite a bit of reflection to help build mentalization. For example, you might say, "It seems to me, it's hard for you to tell me things when . . . Do you suppose that was what was going on?" You might invite the child to try it differently the next time: "Do you think next time you could tell me what was worrying you?"

Robert's mom attunes and then invites reflection:

Robert was supposed to complete his homework before dinner so that he could go to soccer practice that evening. Robert is 13, and he was adopted 2 years ago. In the following vignette, Robert's mom is helping him learn to be accurate with his words:

Mom: (*At the dinner table*) Robert, were you able to finish all your homework? I think you had some math and a language arts sheet, and you were supposed to read a chapter in your novel, is that right?

Robert: (*Head down*) Yeah, I'm done. I can go to soccer practice, right, Mom?

Mom: Yes, Robert, you'll get to go, but I notice that sometimes it's hard for you to tell me that you haven't really finished your homework. I also thought I heard the television on when you were working on your homework. (*Mom is careful with her tone of voice and she uses words that are not accusatory in nature. Her goal is to help Robert trust that it's safe to tell the truth.*)

Robert: I wasn't watching television, Mom. You always think I'm watching television.

Mom: Robert, it's okay. Remember, I love you and want the best for you, right? I know that homework is not your favorite thing—especially reading, right? If you didn't have time to finish all of your work, let's work out a plan so that it gets done and you can go to soccer practice.

Robert: (*After a long pause*) Mom, I didn't read the chapter. It's a stupid book, and I hate it.

Mom: Thanks for telling me, Robert. Did you finish your other assignments?

Robert: Yep, I'll show you (*picks up his math and language arts homework*).

Mom: Great, these look good. Let's read the chapter together when you get home from practice. How does that sound?

Robert: Okay.

LYING TO CONNECT

Some kids with a history of attachment trauma make up stories because there's a hole inside and they feel the need to fill the hole by inventing a story that makes them feel important. This is often the case for children who carry deep-down beliefs that they're invisible, unimportant, or unlovable.

What Can I Do?

Reassure your child that they don't need the story to be connected and loved. Use the phrase, "I'm trying to believe you but I'm having a hard time." Show your interest in something more ordinary.

Jelina's uncle responds with calm attunement:

Jelina, age 10, has experienced a series of relative placements that didn't work out, and she recently came to live with her aunt and uncle. Uncle Able understands that Jelina has a history of telling stories to get attention and that attention gives her a sense of connection. He understands they need to help her find connection in healthy ways. He lets Jelina know in a kind way that he doesn't believe her tall tale, but he provides empathy and invites connection in a healthy way:

119

Uncle Able: How was school today, Jelina?

Jelina: We played softball in PE class. I hit three home runs. I was the star player. Everybody was amazed.

Uncle Able: Jelina, it's okay if you didn't hit three home runs. I love you for just being you.

Jelina: You don't believe me. I'm telling the truth, Uncle Able.

Uncle Able: Honey, I'd love to believe you, but I'm having a hard time with it. Come here and sit with me. Tell me something else you enjoyed today.

Jelina: We got to watch a movie about undersea creatures in science class.

Uncle Able: Now that's interesting. Tell me what you learned.

CONFABULATION RELATED TO FASD

Is there a chance your child was exposed to alcohol in utero? If they were exposed, their made-up stories may be a common symptom called confabulation that's inherent to the FASD brain condition. Kids with FASD are unable to recognize when they're making up a story while it's happening. Shame, lectures, or punishments worsen problems of trust and won't control the problem. Even the most skillful responses may not eliminate the problem due to their brain condition.

What Can I Do?

Remind yourself, "This is a direct result of alcohol in my child's brain in utero. My child doesn't even realize they're lying."

The best strategy for parents of kids with FASD is to stay in their most mentalizing state, free of judgments, connect with the child, and then patiently provide a correction.

Ian's mom connects and then corrects:
Ian's brother told their mom at dinnertime that he overheard Ian, age 14, tell his teacher at school that he'd attended a Chief's football game over the weekend. Mom stays very matter-of-fact and

points out the inaccuracy. Since Ian had shared his story with his teacher, Mom also gently coaches him as to how to make a repair:

Mom: (*Reaching over and placing a hand lightly on Ian's shoulder to connect*) Honey, the story you told Mrs. Smith about attending the football game isn't true. We were home all weekend.

Ian: Oh, yeah. I guess so.

Mom: I know it's hard to stay accurate with your words sometimes. But the right thing to do here is to give Mrs. Smith the true information tomorrow. Just tell her, "Mrs. Smith, my brain got mixed up yesterday. I didn't go to the football game after all." She'll understand. Do you think you can do that?

Ian: Yeah, I can do that.

DEFIANCE

Most parents deal with defiance in their kids from time to time, especially over things they dislike, such as homework, chores, or curfews. For many kids who were traumatized, however, defiance is the norm and cooperation is the anomaly. When they were younger, they learned not to trust adults and developed a very strong, self-protective part of themselves to cope with fear and anxiety by pushing adults away and staying in charge of themselves.

When you attempt to direct or correct your child, the defiance you see is in direct response to your child's assumptions that you're not on their side or you're just being mean. It has not occurred to your child that you're trying to prepare them for adulthood in some way or keep them healthy or safe. They're triggered to high alert very rapidly. As their nervous system moves into the fight-or-flight zone, the younger, self-protective part charges forward automatically.

What Can I Do?

Remind yourself, "My child believes I'm just being mean. I need to help my child understand my intent." Stay calm and attuned. Connect with an empathic response. An affectionate touch may be helpful but attune carefully. If your child's nervous system is already firing, physical closeness may feel threatening. Without lecturing or using too many words, explain the intent of your direction or correction. For example, you might say, "I love you. I'm not asking you to do this to be mean. It's my job to [guide you/ teach you/keep you safe]. I'm on your side."

Darnell's mom shows him that she's on his side:

Darnell, age 16, has lived with his foster parents for the past 2 years. The following situation depicts a conversation in which Darnell has refused to unload the dishwasher. The situation is already escalating a bit because whenever Mom approaches Darnell with a question or comment about chores, Darnell becomes very defensive:

Mom: Darnell, I noticed that the dishwasher is still full of clean dishes.

Darnell: (*Raising his voice*) Why can't one of the younger kids do it? I always have to do everything! I'm sick of this family! When do I get to go to a different foster family?

Mom: (*Stays calm and chooses not to react to Darnell's words or voice tone*) Darnell, I know it's hard to do chores and homework, too. But all you kids have your chores because it's my job as your foster mom to help all of you become responsible adults, and responsible adults are happy adults. (*Next, Mom demonstrates her positive intentions.*) But if you're stressed out today, I'm willing to give you a hand with it. You know, it's okay to ask for help when you're stressed. I'll bet we can knock it out in 5 minutes.

Darnell: (*Shrugs*) Whatever. I guess.

Mom: (*Placing a hand on his shoulder*) How about I'll take care of the silverware while you start on the dishes and glasses?

Darnell: Okay.

STEALING

Kids with a history of nurturing and protection may experiment with stealing a bit, as a way of testing the boundaries or showing off to friends. But many attachment-injured kids exhibit significant stealing behavior. Your child or teen may be stealing very small things on a regular basis or occasionally stealing valuable items, such as technological gadgets or money. They may take things from stores, school, or the homes of friends.

Yes, stealing is against the law, but stealing is also a survival response. If your child cried and no one responded to their needs—whether food, a clean diaper, or touch—they developed the core beliefs of "No one cares" and "I have to be in charge of getting what I need." At a very young age, your child came to believe "I have to take what I can whenever I can." Your child's brain can't distinguish the difference between what they want and what they need, especially when the feelings and perceptions of the younger part of themselves are triggered. The younger child part holds memories of feeling unsafe, unprotected, and deprived. The younger part of them feels deep down that they'll die if they don't get what they think they want or need. Furthermore, kids with an undeveloped prefrontal brain have deficits in their executive functions, which include cause-and-effect thinking, problem solving, and impulse control.

If your child suffers from FASD, your child may steal because of the drive to survive, but also because their brain structure and functioning leave them without the capacity to control their impulses or separate what's theirs from what's not theirs. Personal boundaries and ownership are abstract concepts that just don't make sense to them.

What Can I Do?

In order to remain calm and attuned, remind yourself, "Wants are needs to my child, and my child's downstairs brain is driven to help them survive any way they can. For good reason, my child has a scared younger part that doesn't trust me to meet their needs."

As alarming as stealing can be, a mindful, calm approach is vital to helping your traumatized child feel safe in the present, trust you to meet their needs, and step into their more mature, upstairs, reasoning brain. By building trust and connection, you can calm their nervous system and bring them back to their more mature state. Within their window of tolerance, little by little, you can assist them with thinking things through, managing their impulses, and considering the impact of their actions on others.

An attuned and calm response to your child might be something like:

> It may feel in the moment like you have to take these things to be happy. But I have a hunch that your biggest self knows that the good feelings from taking things don't really last. If you come to me when you have an urge to take something that's not yours, maybe the two of us can figure out something fun we can do together instead.

Mom responds to 9-year-old Elizabeth when she finds lip gloss in her backpack:

Mom: Elizabeth, I was putting some papers in your backpack for school and I noticed some lip gloss. (*Uses the neutral words "I noticed" and a nonconfrontational voice tone*)

Elizabeth: Yeah, I found it.

Mom: (*In a very gentle, soft voice*) Hmm, I was wondering if the lip gloss came from the mall the other day. Remember when we stopped at the mall to get you some new shoes, and we stopped at that bath store and you asked me for some lip gloss? I remember saying no. (*This gentle approach kept Elizabeth's brain regulated so she could continue to participate in the conversation and solve the lip gloss issue.*)

Elizabeth: Yes, I remember, but I found the lip gloss (*looking down and her voice is escalating*).

Mom: (*Knowing that Elizabeth stole the lip gloss, Mom chooses not to engage in a power struggle over whether Elizabeth is telling the truth, but instead to attune to the emotions driving the behavior.*) Elizabeth, I know how much you like lip gloss, and I know it's hard for you when I say no. Remember, we've talked about how the word "no" doesn't mean that you'll never have it and remember that taking things doesn't make you feel good for very long. How about later we return the lip gloss to the store together? We can't take things that are not ours.

Elizabeth: Do we have to?

Mom: Yes, Elizabeth, we do have to. Taking things that are not ours is not legal. It's against all the rules.

Elizabeth: Yeah, okay.

BATHROOM ISSUES

Toilet training can be a challenge, even when a child is in a stable, loving home. Many children in intact homes begin using the toilet regularly and then regress upon starting a new day care or a preschool. Securely attached children who are heavy sleepers can struggle with bed-wetting, sometimes into adolescence. However, early caregiver disruptions and traumatic events can lead to severe bathroom issues that last for years. Children who lived in a chaotic environment or moved from placement to placement before the age of 2 may have missed critical developmental stages when they would have learned how to read their bodies and use the toilet properly.

Some children were not given adequate milk and liquids as infants and developed constipation and started avoiding having bowel movements because it was painful. Some children have a condition in which the colon has stretched so that now there's no urge to have a bowel movement.

Sometimes more severe behaviors, such as playing with feces or urinating in strange places, are related to a traumatic past and dissociative regression to an earlier age of functioning. The bathroom itself may be a trauma trigger for some children. Sometimes in the regressed state, traumatized children who are experiencing intense emotions may go to the bathroom in the corner of a room because they don't know any other way in the moment to express their feelings.

Children who are in a developmentally immature state consistently due to in utero alcohol exposure and an underdeveloped brain may have ongoing problems with controlling urination or bowel movements. They may lack awareness of the physical sensations that indicate they need to use the bathroom. They may even lack awareness that they've wet themselves. The problem may be inherent to their brain condition and unrelated to their traumatic past. However, for kids who have a combination of FASD and attachment trauma, it's likely their bathroom challenges are the result of both developmental trauma and immature development related to FASD.

Children with bathroom problems should be examined by a pediatrician to rule out the possibility of any underlying medical concerns. There are medications that help with nighttime wetting, and a stool softener can help with lack of adequate bowel movements or a stretched colon. An occupational therapist can help with lack of sensitivity to the need to go to the bathroom or to wetness or soiled pants. A physical therapist may be able to help with wetting problems by helping the child to train the muscles that control the bladder.

What Can I Do?

Most children with enuresis (wetting themselves or the bed) or encopresis (uncontrolled bowel movements) have a great deal of shame. To be sure, shaming or punishing kids does not alleviate bathroom issues. Providing incentives and supervising the child as they use the bathroom or clean up after an accident with a patient, calm demeanor can help ensure success. Kids with FASD commonly need incentives, supervision, and assistance throughout their adolescent years. But bathroom issues can be very triggering for parents as no one enjoys bathroom messes, and it becomes particularly challenging with an older child. If your child has bathroom problems, remind yourself, "My child's problem is a common result of an underdeveloped brain and a history of trauma." Following are examples of attuned responses:

- "Honey, I'm here to help you with this. Let's clean this up together."
- "I think this might be about some big feelings you have been experiencing inside. When we go see the counselor tomorrow, maybe they can help us figure out those feelings and help us find a way to talk about them together."
- "Let me show you how to use the toilet paper and how to flush and wash your hands."
- "Dad is going to show you how to aim into the toilet, and then he'll show you what to do next."
- "Honey, let's go over what the doctor told us. A little of this medicine each day will help make your poo softer, so going poo won't hurt anymore. But also, he said it's very important that you spend some time on the toilet each morning before school to give the poo plenty of time to come out. What can we do to make this easier for you? How about we put some of your favorite puzzle magazines in a basket right next to the toilet?"
- "Okay, sweetie, let's remember what the doctor said. No drinks before bedtime and use the bathroom just before bed. But you still might need to go to the bathroom during the night. I know you've been scared about getting up during the night, so I'm leaving the light on in the hall to help. But if you still feel scared, call me and I will help you, okay?"

It will be difficult for your child to change any longtime patterns that have become entrenched. A simple reward chart can be helpful to provide that extra motivation your child needs to keep the changes in the forefront of their mind. For example, you might put up a sticker each time your child uses the bathroom appropriately at specific times of the day. Provide a reward, like a trip to the ice cream parlor together, after your child earns the first six stickers. (To make the goal achievable, do not insist that your child earn the stickers sequentially.) Continue with the reward system until the new pattern has become automatic.

Katie's mother first attunes and then coaches Katie:

Seven-year-old Katie has ongoing issues with wetting herself and not wiping after using the bathroom. Not wiping her bottom has caused some skin irritation and some odor problems:

Mom: Katie, did you remember to wipe?

Katie: (*Doesn't answer and runs outside to play*)

Mom: Come here a second, sweetie. (*Katie comes running. Mom speaks in a quiet voice.*) I just went into the bathroom and noticed that you had forgotten to flush the potty and that there was no toilet paper in there either. I'm wondering about that.

Katie: I did wipe, Mom. I don't know where the toilet paper went.

Mom: Let's do this. Let's have you come back inside for just a minute and we'll make sure you aren't damp. We need to make sure that rash gets better.

Katie: No, I don't want to.

Mom: I know this is hard for you, but it is no big deal. Sometimes it's hard for you to remember to wipe. I'll show you one more time, and you can practice. Let's do it together, and you can go right back out and play. (*It's hard for Mom to stay patient with Katie regarding this issue, so Mom works very hard to stay mindful of her face and voice tone. She's learned that Katie can't learn when the feeling of shame triggers her.*)

Katie: Okay, but I hope this doesn't take forever.

Mom: It won't.

AGGRESSION

Many kids, especially toddlers and preschoolers, occasionally hit or kick, shout, or threaten. Probably few mothers can say their child has never said, "I hate you." However, children and teens with a history of attachment trauma lash out more frequently and with more vehemence than kids raised in more optimal circumstances. Their attachment figures are usually the recipient of their aggression, but siblings, peers, and even teachers may struggle with the child's aggressive behaviors.

Kids who had a chaotic early life are wired for moving into the fight-or-flight zone. If they move into a full-blown meltdown, follow the strategies for the three phases of a meltdown (see Chapter 7). However, if your child is exhibiting brief episodes of lashing out verbally or physically, co-regulation through an attuned response is the most effective response (see Chapter 5).

What Can I Do?

It's extremely challenging to stay calm in the presence of a child having an aggressive episode. Remind yourself, "This is a younger, scared part acting out to feel safe. My child's nervous system is stuck in fight or flight. Their brain and nervous system aren't developed enough for self-regulation."

Intentionally relax your body and your face. Use a calm voice tone. Attune. Appeal to your child's mature state and say, "I get that you're frustrated. Let's pause and sit together for a moment. I know your biggest kid self can handle this. We can solve this problem together."

Take your first opportunity, when your child is operating from their window of tolerance, and invite reflection by simply saying, "I just want to listen so I can understand better."

Safety is a priority. If you need to call the authorities for safety reasons, do so, but let them know your child has a history of trauma and needs a calm approach.

Later on, when your child is within their window of tolerance, invite teamwork to problem solve the situation. Ask, "Can we make a plan for when you get angry? I want to know what you think will help." For example:

- *Ed's plan.* Ed told his parents that he needed to be allowed to go to the basement and be alone when he starts to become angry. Ed said that he could get away from the big feelings by lying on the basement floor and going through his card collections. He also asked for a punching bag in the basement to help him work out the tension in his body when he gets angry.
- *Susan's plan.* Susan and her parents decided to turn her room into a calm space by flanking it with soft blankets, pillows, stuffed animals, favorite magazines, and her CD player with her favorite CDs. Susan found it helpful to bury herself in her animals and blankets and put on her headphones. She had some clay she would pound and mold to help her release the tension in her arms.

Concerning Words

Kids with a history of attachment trauma do not have the ability to express themselves effectively. Your child or teen most likely shouts aggressive words when they're in the fight-or-flight zone—words they don't mean deep down but they help release their big emotions. It's natural to feel hurt, overwhelmed, or angry when your child hurls angry words at you. Try translating your child's verbal onslaught to words that represent what they really mean. This will help you respond with greater attunement to your child's emotional state.

For example, when your child says, "I hate you," translate the words to "I'm angry and hurt." When your child says, "I want to be dead," translate the words to "I feel terrible about myself right now and don't know how to feel better."

Anger as Protection From Vulnerable Feelings

Children who lacked early nurturing dread emotions that make them feel vulnerable. Sadness, grief, loss, hurt, and fear are avoided at all costs. One simple way to avoid those vulnerable feelings is to work up a "mad" feeling to push away the "sad" or the "hurt." Notice if your child tends to get mad when their feelings are hurt, when they have suffered a loss, or when they're anxious about an upcoming event. If this is the case, reassure your child that the sad, hurt, or anxious feelings won't hurt them, that they'll come and they'll go, and that they can come to you and you'll do your best to help.

Evan's mom attunes to his grief:
Ten-year-old Evan spent 2 years in foster care while his mother was working on her recovery from depression and drug addiction. Evan's grandmother died a week ago. Evan's mother recognizes that Evan gets angry and aggressive whenever something happens that is sad:

> **Evan:** I hate you. Get away from me.
>
> **Mom:** Evan, I would like to talk with you for a minute.
>
> **Evan:** No, go away.
>
> **Mom:** Do you know that I'm here for you, no matter what you're feeling? I know that you must be feeling sad about Grandma, and I think you need some more time cuddling and being close to me right now. I want to help you, not fight with you. Will you come snuggle with me? And let's talk about all the fun memories with Grandma. (*Evan moves up onto the couch and lets his mom snuggle with him.*)

Miranda's mom attunes and invites Miranda to problem solve:
Following is a short conversation between 13-year-old Miranda and her adoptive mother. Miranda's reactivity and aggressiveness are related to her mistrust of caregivers. She has a history of early abuse and several changes of foster homes before finding permanency. In this situation, Miranda has asked to go to the mall with her friends, but her mom had to say no because of a previously scheduled doctor's appointment:

Miranda: Mom, my friends and I are going to the mall this afternoon. Will you drop me off at 2:00?

Mom: So your friends are going to the mall, and they want you to come and be there at 2:00? (*Checks to make sure that she understands what Miranda is asking, because Miranda has the belief that her mom never listens to what she says.*)

Miranda: Yep.

Mom: Miranda, I know how much you love going to the mall with your friends. Today we have your physical at 3:00, and my concern is that you would get to the mall and then have to leave again almost immediately. It just doesn't look like that will work out today.

Miranda: (*Begins yelling and tossing her clothes around her room, becoming increasingly agitated*) You never let me do anything! I'm going to the mall! I'll walk! I'm not going to the stupid appointment! I hate you!

Mom: I can see how upset you are, and I know how much you like going to the mall with your friends. It's hard when plans don't work out. Let's sit down and look for a way we can solve this problem.

Miranda: I'm going to the mall whether you take me or not.

Mom: I can see you're still really upset. I'd be happy to work out a solution if we can just sit a minute and talk calmly. Let's use our logical brains to solve this problem.

Miranda: (*Still very agitated; Mom waits quietly.*) What?

Mom: Well, we have the physical, and we have your friends. Let's find a reasonable solution. I can't reschedule the doctor appointment, she's too difficult to get into. I wonder if you could reschedule your friends. I'll bet they'd be willing to get together at the mall on the weekend.

Miranda: They probably won't be able to go.

Mom: Well, we don't know until you ask, right? Let's see what they say.

Miranda: (*Calms down after a short time and makes the calls*)

Note that when Miranda began screaming and throwing her belongings around the room, Mom chose not to address the behaviors but instead attuned to the sad and disappointed feelings Miranda was experiencing. Later on, when Miranda was in a calm state, Mom asked her to sit down so they could talk about what had happened. Mom reminded Miranda that finding ways to calm her brain gives her a healthier brain. They were able to talk about coping skills that could have helped. Miranda agreed to work on taking deep breaths, lying on her bed, and using positive self-talk.

FOOD ISSUES

Like bathroom behaviors, serious food issues are often related to deprivation in early life. Sneaking or stealing food from cupboards and hoarding food are two of the most common behaviors that frustrate parents of children who suffered early deprivation. Stockpiles of candy or other goodies may be found under beds, in closets, or in drawers. If your child hides food, you may be afraid it will cause a bug infestation or rotting food smells. It's important to know that fear of being without food is a hardwired survival response. Children naturally have a heightened fear of starvation when they have experienced a span of time without adequate food. When children have known hunger to a point of fear during early life, that fear becomes entrenched. The desire to hoard, stockpile, and gorge is reflexive and natural—and it is one of the most difficult fears to eliminate.

Another common food issue is gorging on large portions that add extra pounds. Sweet foods or chips or crackers are common foods kids crave that give them a sense of comfort and security. Any of us can get a craving for foods we like, especially when we're stressed or tired. Kids with attachment trauma who have trouble trusting and reaching out for comfort to their parents are especially vulnerable to the use of food to find comfort.

Parents sometimes think their child is oppositional at dinnertime because they refuse to eat what's in front of them and may have a very limited number of foods that they will eat. This actually might be a sign of sensory processing problems that cause sensitivity to certain tastes or textures.

What Can I Do?

Food is core to our survival. Kids who've been hungry at times in their early life are hardwired to fear lack of access to food. Remind yourself, "My child has a younger child part on the inside who didn't have enough. Taking, hiding, or consuming all the food they can is a natural survival response."

Attune to your child's fears that there won't be enough and provide reassurance—over and over and over by saying something like "Sweetie, I think there's a worry about having enough food. I want that worry part to know that at our house there's plenty to eat, and we'll always make sure that you get all the good, healthy food your body needs."

Don't expect complete elimination of this fear. Because it's so hardwired, some anxiety about food may be present forever. It may be helpful to provide some healthy, wrapped items in a special snack basket in your child's bedroom and in your cupboard or refrigerator.

Remind your child that there are healthy snacks available and say something like "Honey, remember, we're eating in just a few minutes. You won't have to wait long. What can you do to keep busy and make the time pass?"

If your child or teen carries extra weight due to overeating, avoid shaming messages. The more shame the child experiences around their urges for food, the more overwhelmed, anxious, and out-of-control the child feels, increasing the need to self-comfort with food. An attuned and reassuring response is much more helpful. For example, you might say,

> "Sweetie, let's think together. What do you think would be a healthy portion? I know it might feel like it won't be enough, but remember, you'll have a snack in 3 hours, and then a short time after that, you will have dinner."

Think of yourself as your child's emotional coach, not the prison warden guarding over the food.

Food refusal and failure to thrive, strange eating habits, and sensory issues related to food textures or tastes often occur in this population of children. Your child's therapists may want to include an occupational therapist and nutritionist as part of the treatment team.

The family therapy and EMDR therapy will help your child develop new ways of managing their emotions, reducing reactivity to food triggers, changing negative beliefs and emotions related to food and traumatic memories, and developing a stronger sense of secure attachment with you. Remember, changing food anxiety is not easy. It's a slow process and requires enormous support and encouragement. Your emotional attunement, empathy, affection, and safety are crucial for helping your child heal trauma-related food issues.

SEXUALIZED BEHAVIORS

Securely attached children within intact families may exhibit some behaviors that could be described as sexual. It's not uncommon for toddlers and preschoolers to begin exploring their own bodies or play doctor and inspect one another's bodies out of natural curiosity. Children of any age may discover good feelings related to touching themselves that subsequently turn into a habit for self-soothing. Typically, younger children can be redirected to another type of soothing activity, and older children can be taught about "private parts" and how to behave modestly.

Sometimes, children with a history of attachment trauma have acquired sexualized behaviors that are not easily redirected. Children who experienced early neglect may have become wired for excessive masturbation because rubbing their own genitals was the only means they had of comforting themselves. When masturbation is a primary method of self-comfort for a young child, the behavior may be entrenched. As the child gets older, the focus on

135

their own genitals may expand to exploring the genitals of other children, or even animals.

Some children in unsafe homes early on witnessed parents behaving sexually or were exposed to pornography or were sexually molested or assaulted. Children's responses to exposure and assault vary widely. Some children are extremely traumatized and act out what happened to them in their play or even with other children. Trauma reenactment is a typical symptom of traumatic stress. The brain attempts to work through the experience this way but gets stuck and continuously plays it through over and over.

For some children, sexual arousal was a good feeling during molestation events that were also confusing and scary. The child may become fixated on reexperiencing the arousal. It's important to remember that their behaviors and compulsions are part of the damage caused by early neglect and abuse.

Kids with FASD are at high risk for sexual reactivity. The regions of the brain responsible for impulse control are underdeveloped, and they lack awareness of personal boundaries. On top of that, they have difficulty understanding the impact of their behaviors on others.

What Can I Do?

The best place to address sexual reactivity is with your child's mental health team. Remind yourself, "This may have been the only kind of touch my child knew"; "My child has an underdeveloped prefrontal brain"; and "My child has stuck, unhealed memories and feelings." Respond to your child's behaviors with connection and attunement. For example, you might say, "We'll work with the therapist on this. We love you no matter what."

Your child's therapist can provide education regarding body parts, privacy, sexual feelings, and boundaries. It's essential to educate without shame, as shame is accompanied by fear, self-hate, and anxiety, which activates their nervous system and sends them into fight-or-flight or shutdown mode.

Of course, safety is the first priority—safety for the sexually reactive child and safety for other children. If you have a sexually reactive child, you won't be able to send your child off to play with others unsupervised. Your child's therapist will help you make a plan to ensure safety for everyone. You'll need to have very clear rules for your sexually reactive child and the other children in the home. For example:

- "One person at a time in the bathroom."
- "The bedroom is a place to play alone, not with others."
- "We don't hide under a blanket with a playmate or sibling or hide together anywhere."
- "We leave our bedroom when dressed appropriately."

Therapy will help your child or teen work through any memories that may underlie the sexualized behaviors and teach your child skills for managing their impulses, self-comfort, and developing healthy relationships with peers. Your emotional support is critical to the process.

In some cases, sexually reactive children or teens have to be placed outside the home for safety reasons and for more intensive therapeutic help. This situation can deepen the child's self-protective defenses and feelings of disconnection unless the parent is intentional about consistent visits and participation in the child's therapy.

Joella's mom responds to her sexually reactive behavior:

Eight-year-old Joella was the victim of sexual abuse in her first home. She'd begun exhibiting some sexualized behaviors in her foster home. Her foster mom was trying to supervise closely but left Joella and her younger 6-year-old brother in the living room for a few minutes while she put a roast in the oven. She walked into the living room to find Joella wrestling around with her brother on the floor:

Mom: Joella, please get off of your brother.

Joella: I'm not doing anything! We're just playing!

Mom: I understand you weren't trying to hurt your brother. But you weren't following the safety rules we talked about in therapy.

Joella: (*Crying*) I wasn't hurting him.

Mom: I know. And I know you love him, but we have to help your brain remember the safe ways to play.

Joella's foster mother set a boundary and then attuned to Joella, reducing her shame and retaining the connection. She knew that this was a therapeutic issue, so she made a good decision to save any further discussion for the therapist's office.

SELF-HARMING AND SUICIDALITY

A 2023 report found suicide to be the second leading cause of death in young people ages 10–24, with the highest rates found in groups of color. Throughout high school students in the United States, 19% had thoughts of suicide, 16% made a plan, and 9% made an attempt (Molock et al., 2023). In a different 2024 report, nonsuicidal self-harming behavior was reported in 16% of kids between 11 and 18 years of age (Farkas et al., 2024).

These rates are alarmingly high. Self-harming and suicidality are associated with trauma, bullying, discrimination experiences, poor family support, depression, anxiety, and other mental health conditions.

What Can I Do?

Your child is at risk even if there's no evidence of self-harming or suicidality due to their difficult past and mental health symptoms. The most important thing you can do to build your child's resilience and decrease their risk is to create safety and connection with you through attunement, empathy, and affection with an open, accepting, demeanor.

If you discover that your child or teen is self-harming or having suicidal thoughts or intentions, work closely with your child's therapist. The therapist will work out a safety plan. Invite connection and trust through attunement and empathy by saying, "I want to understand more about your struggles." Resist the urge to argue with their emotions. Avoid comments such as "You have no reason to feel that way," or "You should be grateful for what you have," or "That's not a big deal." These comments exacerbate feelings of alienation and will shut the door to further connection. Instead, listen extremely carefully and empathize with whatever your child or teen is willing to share.

Finally, ask your child or teen to come to you when they're struggling with thoughts of self-harming or suicide. Ask what they think they most need at those times. Do they need to talk? Do they need to snuggle and be close without talking? Do they need you to help with a distraction? Work out a plan for what they think will best help.

IF YOUR CHILD OR TEEN NEEDS HOSPITALIZATION OR RESIDENTIAL CARE

Sometimes hospitalization or residential care is literally a lifesaver. Sometimes it's needed to stabilize high-risk behaviors, like gang involvement, drug or alcohol abuse, or violent explosions. Sometimes a residential placement can keep the child or teen and others in the household safe and allow parents the relief they need to create a more positive relationship with their child.

Be careful that the out-of-home placement is not presented as a punishment, but as a pathway to safety and healing. Reassure your child or teen you're not going anywhere and that all you want for them is to feel better and be safe. Stay connected through visits, phone calls, and participation in therapy. Listen and empathize.

HOLDING FAST

Children and teens with attachment and trauma issues do not like thinking the way they think or acting the way they act. And yet

139

they have no idea how to change any of it. They don't know it, but their best hope is through an emotionally corrective relationship with you—along with appropriate mental health therapy. Through experiencing you as caring, accepting, trustworthy, and attuned, they can discover what it actually means to feel close to someone. That said, their self-protective defenses will want to kick in at every turn. They'll want the closeness and want to reject the closeness, both at the same time. Let's face it. You'll probably lose your mentalizing state and have to regain it again and again. Don't give up. Step into your mentalizing state and then hold on for the ride. Your persistence will gradually encourage your child or teen to see that the benefits of closeness with you really do outweigh the risks.

List the most challenging behaviors of your child or teen and jot down the attuned responses you'd like to implement:

_____

_____

_____

_____

_____

_____

_____

_____

_____

_____

_____

_____

_____

_____

_____

_____

_____

_____

_____

Chapter 10

Managing Niggling Behaviors Day-to-Day

Kids with a history of attachment trauma have lots of struggles. We've described how to incorporate the building blocks of secure attachment to improve connection, trust, and regulation, as well as addressing those alarming behaviors from a place of attunement and mentalization. Let's look now at strategies to support those day-to-day niggling behaviors without losing sight of the goals of attachment and co-regulation.

Struggles with mistrust, traumatic stress symptoms, depression, and anxiety can leave kids with very little motivation for accomplishing day-to-day tasks and meeting the expectations of grown-ups. Due to trauma during important phases of development, some kids have no idea how to do the things they're supposed to do, like using good manners or taking turns with their siblings. Some kids with brain-based issues can't stay on track without teaching, supervision, assistance, incentives, and regular routines.

OLD-SCHOOL WAYS THAT DON'T WORK

Because of their emotional and behavioral struggles, many attachment-injured kids have received so many scoldings and punishments in their life so far that they've learned to live in shutdown mode in order to not care about how many sentences they'll have to write, how many days they'll be grounded, or how many scoldings they'll get. Other kids continue to care and deal with the scoldings and punishments from the fight-or-flight zone.

The old-school ways can be tempting for two reasons. First, they provide a way to relieve anger and frustration. Second, they actually may stop a behavior for a short time. Unfortunately, however, they also fuel the child's negative beliefs, including "I'm not safe," "I'm bad," and "My parent is bad." They work against attachment security, narrow the child's window of tolerance, and increase the child's mistrust, vigilance, reactivity, and problem behaviors in the long run.

When we fall back on old-school ways, we're generally driven by our feelings of frustration but also by the ways in which we were raised. Most parents find themselves headed down the old-school path at one time or another. The key is catching ourselves, even if we're already on a roll.

Lecturing and Yelling

Lecturing and yelling involves criticism and disapproval. There's no two-way communication or shared reflection. The child or teen is thrust outside of their window of tolerance and their nervous system is firing or shutting down.

Sarcasm

Sarcasm directed toward the child or teen is denigrating. It prevents reflection or two-way communication and either lights up their nervous system or shuts it down.

Shaming

One father said:

> "I thought it was my job to talk sense into Cameron. I thought if I just made Cameron see what he had done wrong, and made him feel guilty about it, he would stop doing some of the crazy lying and stealing. But the more I scolded, the more he shut down. It just drove the wedge between us deeper. I had to learn to stop shaming and just focus on building our relationship—and give the therapy a chance. Now I feel like things are finally getting better between Cameron and me."

For the child or teen, shaming only triggers an overwhelming sense of hopelessness, mistrust, and alienation, leading to depressed mood, anxiety, and shutting down.

Punishments

Punishments are a harsh form of consequences. Punishments leave the child or teen hurt, angry, and disconnected. The survival parts of the brain light up leaving them in the fight-or-flight or shutdown zone.

One mother came in for an initial appointment with her two children. She said, "They'll be fine in the waiting room. They're in the middle of writing 500 sentences each." This mother was not attuned, her kids did not feel a sense of safety or connection, and they were trapped in an endless cycle in which the mother was constantly adding more and more punishments in an effort to make her children behave.

Spanking

You may have been spanked. You may have spanked your children with no harm done. Your neighbors may spank. And yes, spanking usually stops misbehavior immediately. But please, *don't spank.* The positive effect lasts only for as long as the child is fearful. When the fear wears off, the aftereffects include increased mistrust, reactivity, and aggression. Children who are spanked regularly naturally become more and more aggressive over time.

Many parents of traumatized children report that the children "seem to want to be spanked." They push and push until parents finally spank them, and then they "appear fine." But the "fine" is temporary. Children who've been physically abused expect to be spanked and hate the feeling of waiting around for it. It's a relief for them to get it over with. But it activates the survival parts of the brain, fuels aggression, and promotes feelings of alienation and mistrust.

Catching Yourself

If you catch yourself in the middle of any of the old-school ways, use the pause, deep breaths, and self-talk. Reflect on the dominoes. How have you become a trigger? Where can you remove a domino? Develop a new plan. Then, make a repair with your child or teen. You're not giving away power or diminishing yourself in some way by making a repair. You're modeling healthy interpersonal behavior, you're attuning, and you're creating greater attachment security. It's one of the absolute best things you can do for your child and for your relationship.

CONNECT WHILE YOU DIRECT

The key to managing behaviors and helping your child know you're actually on their side, not the enemy looking for ways to make them miserable, is by providing connection while you provide direction. We can provide boundaries and teach appropriate behavior *within* the building blocks of attunement, affection, playfulness, safety, and repairs. Intentional connection keeps the epistemic trust strong and keeps our kids within their window of tolerance. Trust and a calm nervous system are necessary for learning. Siegel and Bryson (2011) explain that making a connection before we direct or correct a child or teen promotes healthy brain integration because the emotional connection activates the emotional centers and the correction activates the centers for reason and logic simultaneously.

The Jobs of Moms and Dads

Chapter 2 described *epistemic trust* as trust that allows us to believe what we're being told is true and meant to be helpful. Kids with a history of attachment trauma who lack epistemic trust assume that their parents say what they say and do what they do just to give them a bad time. It doesn't occur to them that their parents' intentions are good.

One of the family therapy activities in the accompanying clinician's manual (Wesselmann, 2025) is called "The Jobs of Moms and Dads" activity. During this activity, the therapist guides the child or teen in listing the various jobs of parents and what they have to do to accomplish their job as mom or dad.

The list ends up looking something like this:
They keep me safe by insisting . . .

- I buckle my seat belt.
- I look both ways.
- They know my whereabouts.

They keep me healthy by insisting . . .

- I brush my teeth.
- I shower.
- I see the doctor.
- I take medicine if I need it.
- I eat healthily.

They teach me to get along with others by insisting . . .

- I share and take turns.
- I listen.
- I use polite words.

They teach me how to take care of my things so I can live on my own someday by insisting . . .

- I learn to do chores.
- I learn to keep my room clean.
- I learn to be organized.

They provide for my needs, including . . .

- Clothes
- House
- Food
- Transportation

They help me learn things so I can support myself someday and make good decisions by insisting . . .

- I go to school on time.
- I do my homework.
- I cooperate with my teachers.

The old-school response when a child or teen asks "Why?" to any kind of direction or correction is the response "Because I said so." But kids with a difficult attachment history truly don't know the real reasons. They assume their parents' intentions are negative. To increase your child's sense of trust, volunteer the real reasons while connecting with a touch on the shoulder, a quick hug, or a little empathy. You can say, for example:

- "I'll pull out the car at 7:45. I wouldn't want you to be late for school because I know how important school is for your future."
- "Let's hold off on dessert until after we eat our dinner. I know it's really hard to wait sometimes, but it's my job to keep you healthy, you know."
- "Remember, this is your week to take out the garbage. I know it feels like a nuisance, but learning to be responsible with chores helps kids take care of their own homes when they're older."
- "Buckle up, I wouldn't want anything to happen to you!"
- "I'm just doing my mom job (or dad job) to help you be healthy and safe!"

Pre-Teach ("An Ounce of Prevention Is Worth a Pound of Cure")

Most parents can predict which of the day's events are going to be a struggle for their child or teen. All kids have their own unique challenges, but most kids with a history of attachment trauma share some typical difficulties. It's helpful to pre-teach skills for an upcoming event. Pre-teaching is not the same as threatening. The admonition "Don't you dare act up in the waiting room, today—I expect you to be on your best behavior" is *not* pre-teaching, it's a threat. Pre-teaching is most effective when it's done with attunement and empathy for the struggle along with a brief explanation about what's expected. If your child objects, validate their feelings and invite them to problem solve with you. If you include a fun role play with your child or teen, you'll have even more success.

For which of these situations does your child or teen need skills?

- ☐ Holidays and other special days
- ☐ Long car rides
- ☐ Visitors
- ☐ Parent talking on the phone
- ☐ Waiting rooms
- ☐ Checkout lanes stocked with enticing candy and toys
- ☐ Restaurants, especially fancy ones
- ☐ Having other kids over to the house
- ☐ Visiting someone else's house
- ☐ Other: _____

Eight-year-old Becca and her mom go over the "house rules":
Becca's mom decided to go over the house rules and the reasons for the various rules as a little pre-teaching activity before a playdate:

Mom: Becca, I'll bet you're really looking forward to Sarah coming, aren't you? (*Becca nods.*) I'd love to help you have even more fun than usual with Sarah. I know sometimes when Sarah's here, it's really hard not to fight, because you don't always want to play the same things Sarah wants to play. (*Here the mom is empathizing to establish the connection before pre-teaching.*)

Becca: Yeah, she always wants to play house, and I hate playing house. I want to play school.

Mom: Mmm-hmm. It's hard to work things out sometimes. Do you know what the word "compromise" means?

Becca: Yeah, it's when you let the other person get to choose.

Mom: Well, no, that's not it. It means you work out a plan where you each get part of what you want. Like, for instance, we play what you want half the time and we play what I want half the time. Let's practice working out a plan. I'll be Sarah. . . . (*Mom goes on to playfully role-play with Becca and coaches her on how to work out a compromise with Sarah.*)

Children with a history of attachment trauma are way behind their peers in social and emotional skills. Every time you teach, model, practice, and roleplay with your child or teen, you're helping them overcome developmental deficits. If pre-teaching doesn't go well, the negative patterns may be too entrenched to do it on your own. In that case, ask your child's therapist to help you with some pre-teaching for the situations that are typically difficult for your child or teen.

Elephant Problems and Mouse Problems

Kids who are easily triggered have difficulty distinguishing between big problems and little problems. They may become as upset with a little toothpaste on their shirt as they are with accidentally breaking their tablet. Elephant problems and mouse problems are a useful metaphor that all kids can understand.

Fourteen-year-old Tasha and her grandmother address the T-shirt problem:

Tasha: Grandma, I can't find my orange T-shirt.

Grandma: It's still in the dryer. It won't be dry by the time the school bus arrives, you'll have to choose another shirt.

Tasha: Grandma! I want to wear that shirt! (*Throwing her back-pack on the floor*) Jayce is wearing her orange shirt today and we were going to match! I have to wait for my shirt. Can't you drive me to school?

Grandma: I can't take you, Tasha. I have to work this morning.

Tasha: Grandma! (*Falling on the floor dramatically*)

Grandma: Tasha, take a breath. Let's think now. Is this an elephant problem or a mouse problem?

Tasha: (*Grumbling*) A mouse problem.

Grandma: I'm only pointing this out because I love you and I don't want to see you getting your day off to a bad start. Can you do a little problem solving here?

Tasha: (*Getting up*) I guess I'll call Jayce and see if we can do it tomorrow.

If we're going to be successful in teaching our kids the difference between elephant problems and mouse problems, we have to teach *ourselves* the difference. When we're vulnerable due to being tired or overloaded, we are most likely to turn behaviors that are mouse problems into elephant problems. If we're correcting all the mouse problems, we're making corrections constantly.

Make a list of your child's behaviors that are mouse problems:

_____

_____

_____

_____

_____

_____

These problems can be ignored or addressed with a matter-of-fact reminder (along with connecting touch or attunement).

Teaching After the Problem Is Over

After a problem, the situation can be used as a teaching moment as long as you stay connected through attunement, touch, and a soft voice and face, and your child is in the calm window. Teaching does not include the words "I told you so." You can simply identify why the behavior was problematic and what would work better the next time. The less emotion involved, the easier it will be for your child to take it in. Remember that epistemic trust is a requirement for learning.

If your child's nervous system is activated, begin with some calming, co-regulating strategies. Don't try to begin teaching until you've gained a connection.

Eight-year-old Steven and his parents:

Steven's parents were embarrassed when he became reactive to his grandmother at dinner over a serving of peas. Dad touched Steven's hand and whispered, "Take a deep breath. Remember, we talk with one another to work out our problems." Steven remained agitated but did not melt down. That night, when Steven was in bed, his dad sat down on the bed and went over the event:

> "Steven, I know you don't like peas, and you felt upset when Grandma asked you to eat your peas. Let's come up with a plan for what you can say to Grandma next time. If we come up with a plan, we can prevent the mouse problem from turning into an elephant problem, right?"

Together, they talked about how Steven could mention that peas are "not my favorite," and ask, "Would it be okay if I just try a small bite?" At the end, his dad praised Steven for working on a plan and using his "smart thinking brain."

Effective parents are teachers. Don't expect to teach any concept just one time. Learning requires repetition, and for kids with developmental deficits or brain differences, even more repetition is required. Connection, attunement, and playfulness will keep your child or teen in the calm window where learning is possible.

Offering Choices

Kids with a history of attachment trauma often look for ways to find control in their life because they started out life unsafe and powerless to do anything about it. When kids are controlling, parents often naturally try to get in the driver's seat by exerting extra control, which only triggers the child's traumatic past. When we find ways to offer simple choices in the moment, kids feel a sense of control and they feel heard and we can still hold on to rules and expectations. For example, if the rule is "Children get ready for bed at 8:00," we can give lots of choices around that rule in terms of what pajamas to wear, whether the child takes a shower or a bath, whether to read or just talk at bedtime, and whether to brush teeth before or after the shower. If the rule is "Chores done before dinner," parents can offer a choice in terms of whether to empty or load the dishwasher or whether to bag up the trash or take it to the curb. Choices teach cooperation, decision making, and flexibility—all healthy qualities for life.

Brendon's dad gives choices:

In the following conversation, Brendon's dad helps 14-year-old Brendon use his "thinking brain" by offering him choices. Brendon had brought home a low grade on an algebra test to be signed by his parents. He was visibly upset about the grade:

Dad: Brendon, I know you don't feel good about this grade. Let's do some problem solving about how you get some help with algebra and get your grade up.

Brendon: I can get it up, Dad. I don't want to talk about it.

Dad: Brendon, it's okay, I understand. (*Dad touches Brendon's shoulder.*) How about we talk either after dinner or before bed?

Brendon: Oh, okay, we can talk about it after dinner.

Brendon's dad was quite skillful in that he empathized right away with his son and respected his need to have some space. By giving him a choice about times to talk, it gave Brendon a sense that he did have some control and allowed for Brendon to become a more collaborative partner in the discussion later.

Some children become confused and anxious in the face of choices, especially if parents offer too many choices and complex explanations. Kids with FASD or ASD, or who are developmentally younger due to early trauma, may become easily overwhelmed by choices. Keep the choices simple, and if you observe the child becoming overwhelmed, take a pause, connect, and then give a simple suggestion starting with "Hmm, I wonder about this idea . . . "

Talking Through Problems With the Help of Active Listening

When there's a problem, attune with empathy and an open, curious mind to help your child or teen feel safe and connected. You might say, "Help me understand. . . . " Active listening is a way to attune and help your child or teen feel heard and understood. *Active listening* involves clarifying whatever your child or teen says to make sure you've got it right. When kids feel heard this way, they're much more willing to walk through the problem with you to find a solution. Psychologist Ross Greene (2021, p. 85) suggests that it's best to repeat back exactly what our kids say instead of paraphrasing to make absolutely certain they feel heard. No matter what your child or teen says, don't jump into arguments about why your child is in the wrong. Repeat it back and clarify what you heard to make sure you understand. Once they feel understood and trust that your intentions are to be helpful, you can share your point of view by saying, "Here are my concerns . . . " and "Let's see if we can find a solution that will help with your concerns and my concerns." Avoid acting like the expert with all the answers. It's much more collaborative to offer ideas a little tentatively. For example, you might say, "Hmm, I'm just wondering if it might work to do a little of this room organizing tonight, and then wait and finish it off tomorrow." Greene (p. 75) explains that collaboration invites cooperation. Karen Purvis and colleagues (2007) suggest that listening, negotiating, and finding compromises builds trust and connection.

Again, attune to your child's capacity to understand compromises. Kids who are developmentally young or have brain-based challenges, such as ASD or FASD, may become overstimulated and overwhelmed with the complexity of negotiating a compromise. They may respond better to a simple offer of a solution with attunement and empathy for their feelings.

Who Has the Floor?

A helpful way to engage your child or teen in a discussion of a topic that tends to cause frustration for either of you is with the activity "Who Has the Floor?" (This activity is described in the clinician's guide [Wesselmann, 2025] as a family therapy activity, but it's easy to implement at home as long as parents stay attuned and playful.) Pick up a pen and announce that the pen is a microphone. Say, "Whoever holds the microphone gets to talk about their point of view. Then the other person gets the mic and repeats what they heard before they share *their* point of view." Most kids are intrigued by using the pen as a microphone and are willing to participate, as long as they're in a calm state. Once both you and your child feel heard, you can set aside the pen and invite your child to help you come up with solutions.

Fifteen-year-old Roger and his aunt address a problem:

Aunt Libby: Roger, see this pen here? This pen is a microphone. Whoever holds the pen gets to talk, but we'll take turns with it. Whoever listens has to check out if they heard everything correctly, okay?

Roger: What are we going to talk about?

Aunt Libby: Well, you've been getting angry when I remind you about homework time.

Roger: I don't like doing homework right after dinner! I always get it done, anyway.

Aunt Libby: Here's the pen. You get to go first. I'll listen hard to your feelings about this, and I'll check with you to see if I have it right, okay?

Roger: (*Taking the pen*) I don't have that much to say. I get my homework done every night. I don't see that there's a problem.

Aunt Libby: (*Taking the pen*) You think things are fine because you get your homework done.

Roger: Yep, that's right.

Aunt Libby: Okay, my turn. I'm worried because it's my job to see to it that you're healthy. I'm afraid you'll end up sick, because you don't get to your homework until 9:30 at night. And you're really grouchy and exhausted in the mornings. It's not good. (*Hands Roger the pen.*)

Roger: (*Taking the pen*) You're worried I'm gonna get sick and you hate when I'm grouchy.

Aunt Libby: Close enough. Can we brainstorm some solutions that'll make us both happy? (*Roger shrugs*) Okay, I'll start. Let's see, I could take a cot to school so you can nap over lunch.

Roger: I'd be okay with that!

Aunt Libby: Hmm, your principal might not like that idea, though. Do you have any better ideas?

Roger: Mmm, I suppose I could set an alarm on my phone for 8:30 and start my homework then.

Aunt Libby: I like that idea a lot!

Fourteen-year-old Frank and his dad:

In the following conversation, Frank's dad skillfully implements active listening and co-regulation. Frank had entered the house after school and slammed his backpack onto the kitchen counter:

Dad: (*Calmly*) I notice that you're really upset. Can you help me understand?

Frank: (*Shouting*) That stupid history test was too hard! I'm not retaking that stupid test!

Dad: The test was stupid and hard and you didn't pass and you don't want to retake it. (*Invites Frank to sit down and have a snack with him*) I love you, son. I know it's a pain to do a retake, but I know giving up on it won't make you feel very good, either. Do you want milk with those cookies? Let's just relax a bit and talk about other things. Then who knows? Maybe later we could come up with a plan for how to master that darn history test.

Frank's dad attunes and empathizes with his son to connect and calm Frank's brain. Later, Frank's dad will invite him to find a solution together.

Eight-year-old Rhonda and her mom address an earlier problem:
Rhonda's mother uses active listening to help Rhonda mentalize her thoughts and feelings about a problem situation. After that, they work on a solution together:

Mom: (*First gives Rhonda a hug to connect with her*) Rhonda, you were really struggling in church today, and I feel bad that we didn't have a good time together. Let's put on our detective hats and see if we can figure out what went wrong.

Rhonda: I don't know, I guess I just got mad.

Mom: Yes, you did get mad, didn't you? I wonder what triggered your mad feelings today.

Rhonda: I think I didn't like it that Lori was sitting on your lap at church.

Mom: Oh, you didn't like Lori sitting on my lap. But that was before the service started. Were you holding in mad feelings all that time?

Rhonda: Well, and then you had your arm around her.

Mom: Oh, then I had my arm around her? So were you thinking I didn't love you, and I loved her because I had my arm around her then?

Rhonda: (*Crying now*) Yes, I always think you love her more. She's always good, and I'm always bad.

Mom: Rhonda, I love you so much. You're lovable and good. Come here, let's snuggle a little bit and work out how you can tell me the next time you start feeling unloved.

Connect and Redirect Quickly in the Moment

When you're observing a behavior that you want to interrupt quickly, you'll want to connect with your child or teen quickly. A quick connection can be achieved through an attuned, empathic statement and a quick affectionate hug, a light touch on the arm, or an invitation for your child to come and sit close. The connection can also be quickly achieved through verbal affirmations, such as "Remember, I love you" or "You know, you're really special."

Redirection can be accomplished by a simple "I notice . . . " and a quick reminder of the expectation. If your child or teen has difficulty processing information, you may need confirmation that they understand.

Vicki gives a quick connect/redirect:

Vicki: Honey (*giving 7-year-old Danny a quick hug*), I notice that your toys are still on the floor. Remember the rule for when you finish playing with your toys? I'll bet it only takes you a minute. (*Waits for Danny to start his job before she leaves the room.*)

Vicki connects and redirects effectively again:

Vicki: Hey, Danny, love you! (*She gives a quick side hug*) I notice that your voice is very loud right now, and I'm concerned it may disturb the other people here in the restaurant. Please practice using your inside voice—like this (*speaks softly to demonstrate*). Okay, can you do it? Let me hear you try.

INCENTIVES

Kids who have trouble staying on task due to ADHD or other brain challenges may respond well to on-the-spot positive incentives to help them focus, follow a direction, or complete a task. This type of incentive does not have to be big, but it should be immediate. For example, the parent might mention that there'll be time for an extra bedtime story if the child gets their room picked up quickly. The parent might offer to allow the child to play on the tablet "as soon as" they get their seat belt buckled. A child might get a piggyback ride to the car if they can get their coat on quickly. A teen might get to hang out with friends "as soon as" their homework is done or earn some extra allowance by helping dad in the garage.

A reward system can be put in place long term to help with shaping a behavior that's been a struggle. However, there are three mistakes parents often make:

- *Mistake 1.* The reward system is so complicated that it's confusing to the child or teen and even confusing to the parent. It's too hard to predict when they'll get rewards and when they won't.
- *Mistake 2.* The system is set up to reward vague "good behavior." This feels very random and again confusing to the child or teen.
- *Mistake 3.* The reward system is too frustrating because the expectations are unrealistic. Commonly, parents insist that the child or teen behave in the desired way for several days "in a row" to earn the reward. Can any of us remember a time when we tried to diet, exercise regularly, or give up smoking or some other habit and succeeded immediately for a whole series of days?
- *Mistake 4.* The reward system is successful but then it's removed too soon and the child backslides. It's unrealistic to expect long-term change through a short-term intervention.

In any of these situations, the child or teen will become increasingly anxious or shut down.

Good rules of thumb are:

1. *Keep it simple.* Target just one or maybe two behaviors.
2. *Keep it specific.* Target specific behaviors, such as "getting dressed for school on time" or "getting homework done by 7:00."
3. *Make it achievable.* Choose a behavior that you know your child is capable of achieving so that they're rewarded sooner rather than later. If a sticker or token system is used, allow the child to earn a small item for achieving, say, five

stickers—but not in a row. Remember, it's a process of grad-ually moving your child toward the desired goals.

4. *Keep it going until the habit is well ingrained.*

Some kids with FASD, ASD, or trauma-related developmental def-icits don't respond well to a reward system because they're too concrete and they lack cause-and-effect thinking or they're unable to visualize the reward and keep it in mind. If it's not working, don't continue the system. Some kids respond well with intermit-tent reminders. But remember, they may still become frustrated with the task and need hands-on help, especially when the task requires organization, problem solving, or focus that is difficult due to their underdeveloped prefrontal brain.

Following are two examples of the use of simple reward systems for specific behaviors:

- Peter (age 10) was developmentally delayed and suffered from a history of abuse and neglect prior to coming to Beth's home as a foster child when he was 4. With help from the therapist, Beth set up a simple reward system with Peter. She gave him a star sticker each morning that he was tantrum-free before school and each evening that he was tantrum-free. When he had earned two stars, she allowed him to choose a small prize from a prize box. This approach continued until Peter was tantrum-free most of the time. Next, Peter's mom started a reward system to motivate Peter to pick up his toys before bed each night.
- Gabe and Ann set up a simple reward system for 14-year-old Angela. Each night after completing her homework, she was given a point, and when she'd earned 5 points, she was allowed to invite a friend to spend the night. They continued the system until she was in the habit of doing homework on a regular basis, and then they set up a new system to encourage her to help with dishes each night.

Consequences: Should I or Shouldn't I?

When parents use consequences in a state of frustration or anger, the consequence is typically communicated with anger, shame, or sarcasm. Kids who were protected and nurtured in their early years might be able to tolerate their parents' anger once in a while. But kids who felt unprotected and unloved in early life are thrust into the fight-or-flight zone and view their parents as against them. Furthermore, harsh consequences are much less effective than mild consequences. Writing 100 sentences, being grounded for a month, or confinement to their room for hours leaves kids convinced that no one cares. The beliefs they learned in early life, such as "I'm bad" and "You're mean," are deepened. Harsh consequences along with anger worsen mood, attachment problems, and traumatic stress.

If the parent has a calm demeanor and communicates the consequence within the building blocks of attunement and empathy, occasional negative consequences may reduce some challenging behaviors if they're used only occasionally and if they're mild. It's always best if a negative consequence can be tied logically to the problem behavior. For example, "A little calming downtime will help you slow down so you can think and manage better," or "An apology note will help fix things."

Your empathy delivers the message "I care about you" and helps retain the epistemic trust and safety that allows your child or teen to take in the information you want them to learn. Cline and Fay (2006) promote judicious use of negative consequences that are logical and accompanied by empathy to improve the relationship and reduce power struggles. Helping your child or teen sense your compassion helps them trust you're on their side and want the best for them.

As you talk with your child or teen about the issue, pay attention to any irritation you feel and manage it with a pause, some breaths, and some self-talk. Empathize with words like "I know it's hard to be a kid sometimes," or "I know it's hard to remember the rules," whether you're asking them to sit quietly for a few minutes or removing their TV privileges for the evening. Remind them that you love them and you have confidence they can remember and do better next time. Connect with affection through a little side hug or a touch on the arm. Soften your face, your eyes, and your voice. Use a matter-of-fact or soft tone of voice, without sarcasm or anger. Stay affectionate, even if you're being firm. Remind your child or teen of the reason you want them to learn whatever it is you want them to learn (see the earlier section on "The Jobs of Moms and Dads").

For kids with FASD, the use of negative consequences can be completely ineffective because their prefrontal brain is missing the structures necessary for impulse control and cause-and-effect thinking and their memory is impaired. If your child with FASD is struggling with a certain task or behavior, it may mean they need more assistance from you.

The triangle in Figure 10.1 provides an overall picture of the integrative strategies for parents raising kids affected by attachment trauma. The foundation for everything includes the build-

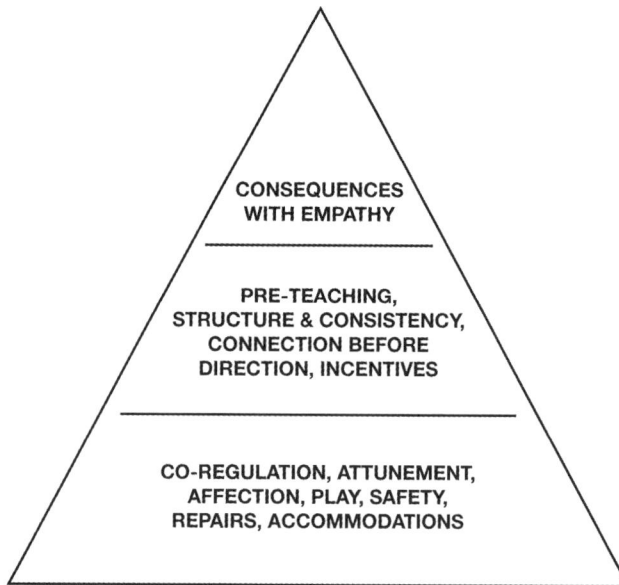

FIGURE 10.1 Integrative Strategies Triangle

ing blocks for attachment security, trust, and connection along with accommodations to assist kids with what they can't do on their own. On top of that, kids need structure, consistency, preteaching, and direction. Consequences (mild) with empathy are used very sparingly and therefore they're the smallest piece of the triangle at the top.

Uncle Trey ineffectively gives a consequence to 14-year-old Bobby:

Uncle Trey: I let you use my tools yesterday and look what I found lying in the driveway. When will you learn that I mean it when I tell you to put my tools away after you use them? You're grounded from watching any TV for the rest of the week.

Bobby: But it's not fair! I'm going to be totally bored after dinner.

Uncle Trey: (*With a sarcastic tone of voice*) Well, isn't that too bad.

Bobby: I hate you! I hate living here!

In this situation, Bobby ends up thinking about what a mean uncle he has and doesn't even remember what he did that resulted in being punished.

Uncle Trey learned how to effectively give a consequence from Bobby's therapist:

Uncle Trey: Bobby, I just found my tools lying in the driveway. Look, son, I know it's hard to remember rules sometimes. The rule about putting tools away is really important to me, because my good tools are quite expensive. I'm sorry, I know it's hard, but I'm going to have to remove your computer privileges for today as a consequence. Please try to remember next time, okay?

Bobby: But I'll be bored tonight! I don't know what to do after dinner.

Uncle Trey: Bobby, I'm sorry, I know consequences can be hard to deal with sometimes. I'm just trying to help you learn how to be responsible, because that's my job.

In this situation, Bobby is left feeling frustrated with himself for leaving the tools out, and he makes a resolution to remember the tools' rule the next time.

Write down two or three empathic statements that you would feel comfortable using when you give a consequence:

1. _____
   _____
2. _____
   _____
3. _____
   _____

It is not easy to develop the habit of using empathic statements, so you will have to stay mindful and intentional with this new practice. Discuss the plan with your partner to make sure you are parenting as a team.

Brief Lines for "Mouse" Behaviors

Remember that minor undesirable behaviors should go into the *mouse problems* basket and be ignored or addressed with a low-key, matter-of-fact approach. Following are some brief lines that can be quite effective. All of these lines should be said with a loving facial expression and a calm voice, along with a hug or a hand on the shoulder to connect.

- "I love you too much to argue." This line is recommended by Cline and Fay (2006, p. 65). It's a wonderful line for ending an argument before it starts, and it conveys the belief that an argument would not be good for your child or teen. If your child keeps arguing, walk away. Be sure to engage your child in normal social conversation whenever you can. Listen and show interest in what your child has to say to reinforce the nonarguing methods of engaging with you.
- "I'm trying to believe you, but I'm having a hard time." This is a wonderful line because it avoids reinforcing the lying behavior by

arguing about whether it's true or not. In just this one brief comment, you're letting your child or teen know that you'd like to give them the benefit of the doubt, you do suspect they're not being truthful, and it would mean a lot if they were honest. Another version of the line is "I would like to believe that," followed by busily moving on to something else. Either line avoids a power struggle and makes it clear to your child that you're moving on and that the lying behavior is the child's problem, not yours.

- "You know the rules." This line can be used for many small behaviors. The line makes it clear to your child that you've noticed the behavior without reinforcing the behavior by excessive attention or arguing. A loving hand on the shoulder and a loving face helps keep the connection. If you believe the behavior warrants a consequence, you might add, "I'm giving you this one reminder." It keeps you out of lecturing or arguing and keeps the behavior as your child's problem, not yours.

- "I notice . . . " It's worth re-mentioning that when your child breaks a rule, it's best to point it out by just "noticing" it. For example: "Sweetheart, I notice you left your shoes in the middle of the floor." Use a pleasant tone of voice to redirect: "Remember the rule—shoes in the closet." Then supervise to make sure your child follows through.

Grandfather treats Grey's sneaking behavior as a mouse problem:

Grandpa Bill was frustrated with his 14-year-old grandson Grey because Grey was sneaking extra video/computer playtime whenever he had the chance. Each time Grandpa caught Grey sneaking off to his room with a handheld game or getting on a computer game when he was supposed to be doing homework, Grandpa sat Grey down and explained why the rules were important and why he was losing trust in Grey. Then he interrogated Grey as to why he was choosing to defy the rules regarding use of the games. Grandpa tried many consequences, from grounding to removal of privileges. He grew angrier and angrier. The family therapist suggested to Grandpa that instead of lecturing or using consequences, he might try treating the sneaking behavior as a mouse problem and simply say, "You know the rules." He suggested that Grandpa present a loving face and a soft voice to maintain the relationship, while holding out his hand for the game or signaling Grey to get back to his homework. The therapist suggested that Grandpa walk away quickly after a very brief intervention. Grandpa found there was much less drama around the incidents and he and Grey were able to engage in more playful interactions. Gradually, the sneaking behaviors reduced.

A Note About Screen Time

Kids who lack secure attachment and struggle with feeling alone or disconnected can easily get hooked on screen time. Time with screens is passive time. It has its own built-in rewards with no expectations from others and no relationship triggers with which to contend. On the positive side, cell phones, video games, and computers are a way teens and older children connect and make friendships in the current culture, especially teens and older kids. On the negative side, too much time on screens can interfere with emotional and social development. Time with others, playing games, drawing or painting, using clay, making things with paper and glue, riding bikes, shooting hoops—these types of activities are the best way to encourage creative self-expression and interpersonal skills.

Talk to your child's pediatrician or therapist about the appropriate amount of time that might be acceptable for your child to be on screens considering age and development. Create structure around screen time that your child or teen can depend on each day to reduce conflict in this area. Many families have a rule that all phones go on their chargers during meals and at a set time each evening. Most families engage in some video game use, which is fine, but it works best if there's some structure to the time and a plan for games to be used in a space where family members can play together, versus located in the child's bedroom where it becomes a solitary activity.

Chapter 11

Improving Your Own Life

PARENTING IS HARD. Parenting children with challenging behaviors related to attachment or trauma issues is megahard. By now, you've begun implementing strategies for helping your child, but you may be asking yourself, "How can I stop doing the wrong things? Before I know it, I find myself yelling and lecturing." You may be thinking, "Now that I know what I *should* be doing to help my child, I feel worse about myself when I don't do it."

Being the kind of parent you most want to be means taking care of yourself first and foremost. If your energy and zest for life have "gone missing," you're lacking the internal resources you need to be emotionally present for any significant others in your life, but especially for your child with high needs. It's time to take an inventory of what's depleting you emotionally or physically and then problem solve those situations. You may not be able to help the way you feel right now this minute but you can make changes in your lifestyle and routine that bring back feelings of joy and happiness you forgot existed.

TAKE AN INVENTORY

The first step is to take a thorough inventory of the parts of your life that are depleting you of the internal resources you need for happiness and health.

Check any of these stressors that pertain to you (in addition to the stress of raising your child):

- ☐ Lack of sleep, for any reason
- ☐ Pain or illness of any kind
- ☐ Recent loss of any kind
- ☐ Interpersonal conflict
- ☐ Financial worries
- ☐ Loneliness and isolation
- ☐ Working excessive hours
- ☐ Extra demands on time and resources for any reason
- ☐ Demands from other children, older parents, or other family members
- ☐ Major change, such as a move, a new job, or a new relationship
- ☐ Active addictions
- ☐ An emotional disorder/chemical imbalance
- ☐ Your own trauma history, including childhood experiences of abuse or neglect
- ☐ Other: _____

Look over the items you checked and star any items you could begin addressing right now. For example, you might make an appointment with your doctor for pain, illness, or sleep problems. You could make an appointment with a financial advisor about debt. You could make an appointment with a therapist to resolve conflicts or past trauma.

WORK WITH YOUR BODY

Get acquainted with your body and the signs in your body that your nervous system is becoming activated.

Check any of the following clues to distress held in your body:

- ☐ Tension or pain in neck, shoulders, or back
- ☐ Nausea or stomachache
- ☐ Headache

☐ Chest tightness or shallow breath
☐ Tension in jaw
☐ Other: _____

Open your mind to practices that can help calm your nervous system and help you find more pleasure and satisfaction in your life. Yoga, meditation, or prayer can calm your brain and increase your capacity for mindful self-awareness. Walking, exercise classes, or hobbies can lower your felt stress, increase feelings of pleasure, and expand your window of tolerance. Prayer, spiritual books, study groups, or church/temple involvement can help you look deeper into the meaning and purpose of your life, increase your faith in something greater than yourself, and help you find greater serenity and optimism for life.

Find a phrase or "mantra" that you can use on a regular basis. A *mantra* is a word or phrase that you find uplifting or inspiring. For example, a mantra might be "Let go, let God," or the words "One day at a time." Write your mantra on sticky notes and place them on your bedroom mirror, on the refrigerator, and in the car. Incorporate your mantra into passwords on your computer.

Practice paying attention to the signs of nervous system activation in your body. Step away from what you're doing and use a method of self-calming that you enjoy. For example:

• Focus on the disturbance in your body while thinking of your mantra. Take some very deep breaths followed by long, slow exhalations.
• Pendulate (a strategy created by Peter Levine, 2010) by paying attention to the physical disturbance and then paying attention to a part of your body that feels comfortable. Continue alternating your focus back-and-forth between the disturbance and the place of comfort.
• Bring up in your mind an individual from your life or from movies or books or history who inspires you in some way. Imagine that individual is right next to you supporting you. What message might they have for you?

• Picture yourself relaxing in a fantasy place that is soothing and relaxing to you. Notice what you can see there—what you might smell, touch, and hear in that place.

You may have other favorite ways to calm your nervous system. Practice whatever you find most helpful to you.

REACH OUT

Community, connections, and support networks support a calm nervous system and emotional well-being. Join parent groups or adoptive or foster parent organizations and attend their social events, group meetings, or conferences. Or reach out to other worried or stressed parents you know and see if there's interest in forming a book club to study relevant books. If you are spiritual, consider joining a community of individuals who share your faith if you haven't already. Make contacts with old friends and start meeting for lunch.

Look into getting help with your kids through a local respite service (a service that specializes in providing relief for parents of challenging children) or find trustworthy friends or relatives who are willing to help. Some parents set up respite or childcare for a few hours a week or for a weekend every month. Respite gives parents needed space to recharge their energy and regain perspective. Regular respite also gives partners time to pay attention to each other and nurture their relationship. Respite care won't damage your relationship with your kids—it will enhance it.

COUPLE ISSUES

Staying connected as a couple can be a real challenge when partners are raising a child or teen with trauma and attachment problems. Each partner is looking to the other for support, for reassurance, and for answers, and each parent simultaneously feels emotionally depleted and unable to be supportive to the other. In addition, parents often come from different backgrounds and have different styles of parenting, and yet neither parent may be feeling effective. Naturally, parents easily fall into patterns of arguing.

If you have a partner and your relationship is stressed, reading this book together may help you get on the same page in responding to your child or teen. Try to sit down together and discuss what you've read. Talk about how you can support each other and strengthen your relationship despite the stress in your household. Make date nights a priority, with help from a respite provider, family, or friend. Make it a point to talk and share each day after the children are in bed or make lunch dates together on school days.

Consider some sessions with a couple counselor to improve your style of communication, reduce conflicts, and learn how to become mutually supportive. Consider asking your child's therapist for help finding an appropriate provider. A stronger relationship between you and your partner will increase your resilience as individuals and will provide a more secure environment for your child.

EXTENDED FAMILY ISSUES

Many families participating in therapy with their child or teen struggle with extended family members who don't understand attachment trauma. Frequently, extended family give advice, such as "Give him a good spanking," "Stop spoiling her," or "Teach him some manners." The extended family may tell the parents to place the child elsewhere, remove the child from their medications, or give the child more medications. Extended family members may minimize the difficulties and accuse parents of exaggerating them.

It may be helpful to give extended family members this book to read, or it may be helpful to sit down and talk directly with them about how they can be helpful. Remind yourself that *you* are the child's parent, and that your extended family members don't know what they don't know.

Check the responses that may help you the next time you have conflict with any of your extended family members:

- ☐ "I know you're coming from a place of care and concern for us, but I want to reassure you that we have some good support and advice that we're following."
- ☐ "I know it's hard to understand, but our child came to us with some emotional injuries that we're trying to heal. It would be most helpful to us if you could try to stay positive."
- ☐ "I've been learning that these behaviors are driven by early trauma and attachment problems. We're working on improving trust and calming our child's nervous system. The old-school methods just aren't helpful."

STUCK EMOTIONS

Many parents don't realize that they're suffering from grief. You may be grieving due to losses you've experienced since your child joined your family. You may be grieving loss of control, loss of alone time, time with friends, or couple time. You may have unresolved grief related to infertility. You may be mourning for the fantasy family you'd imagined long ago. You may have suffered major losses of parents or others in your life.

You may be struggling with perfectionism. Chapter 6 closes with the Voltaire saying, "Perfect is the enemy of the good." A truer statement was never said. Don't let perfectionism ruin your fun. Don't let it drive you to overfocus on achievements or what others might be thinking. Don't let it get in the way of enjoying your child's quirks and uniqueness. Don't let it make you inflexible.

You may have come to believe that you didn't measure up when you were a kid. You may have been taught that appearances were everything and that achievements were the only way to prove yourself worthy. You may have learned the only way to stay out of the line of fire of criticism was to avoid mistakes and conform to expectations at all costs.

You may have experienced troubling events in childhood that are triggered consciously or subconsciously when you're with your own child today. For example, sitting down to dinner with your kids may trigger the best and the worst memories of sitting down to dinner with your parents when you were young. Watching your child march off to school may trigger memories of your favorite teachers or your worst teachers. Watching your child enjoy their ninth birthday party may trigger memories related to turning nine. If you have a large number of distressing childhood memories, you're at risk for experiencing triggers in many day-to-day situations.

Think a little more in depth about your childhood . . . (answer yes or no):

- Did you consider your parents warm and loving? _____
- Was it an environment where you could share your feelings openly? _____
- Could you talk about things that troubled you? _____

If you answered the above questions with a yes, the strategies you're learning will come more naturally to you. If you identify with the following situations, however, it would be natural for you to struggle with triggers . . . (answer yes or no):

- Did you grow up in a home where children were to be seen and not heard? _____
- Were your problems dismissed as unimportant? _____
- Were you criticized, rejected, or shamed? _____
- Did you experience early separations or losses? _____
- Were you physically or sexually abused? _____
- Did you experience physical or emotional neglect? _____
- Did you have a parent who suffered from severe mental illness or addiction? _____
- Was there significant fighting in your home? _____

ADULT ATTACHMENT PATTERNS

In Chapter 1, we described two adaptations kids make when they're unable to rely on their parents to respond to their needs. When the environment doesn't provide enough attunement and empathy, kids naturally lean toward the ambivalent-resistant attachment pattern, expressing their needs and feelings with intensity in order to be heard. When the adults around them are uncomfortable with their feelings and needs, kids naturally lean toward the avoidant attachment pattern, shutting down feelings and needs for closeness.

Early attachment researcher Eric Hesse (1999) identified adulthood attachment patterns that correlate with the childhood patterns. An ambivalent-resistant pattern in childhood tends to move into a "preoccupied pattern" in adulthood. Feelings and needs are expressed with intensity due to strong feelings of anxiety. An avoidant pattern in childhood tends to move into a "dismissive" pattern in adulthood. Feelings and closeness are avoided as a defense to underlying anxiety. A third label, "unresolved/disorganized," indicates some unresolved loss or abuse. Feelings carried from childhood can be easily triggered.

The secure attachment pattern for adults indicates a healthy level of comfort in close relationships. There's typically an easy feeling with both giving and receiving affection.

Attachment patterns aren't black and white. We may have mild tendencies one way or another. We may have mild or strong tendencies for more than one pattern. Unfortunately, it's difficult for us to know definitively what our patterns are, because others can usually see tendencies in us that we don't see. But the labels really aren't important. As you consider the following questions, the goal is simply to recognize attitudes you may have carried forward from childhood but wish to change. Try to stay curious, nonjudgmental, and open to new insights:

How true are each of the following statements?

	A little true	Quite true	Very true	
1.	—	—	—	"I'm uncomfortable spending too much time snuggling."
2.	—	—	—	"I feel awkward expressing feelings of love with words."
3.	—	—	—	"I don't want to need anyone."
4.	—	—	—	"I don't like showing my emotions."
5.	—	—	—	"I never feel like I can get enough closeness from others."
6.	—	—	—	"I have to push others to be responsive to my needs."
7.	—	—	—	"Feelings of rejection or exclusion are excruciating to me."
8.	—	—	—	"I have intense negative emotions about my childhood."
9.	—	—	—	"I get overwhelmed and can't verbalize painful memories."
10.	—	—	—	"I enjoy snuggling and being close with my partner."
11.	—	—	—	"Relationships are a source of satisfaction in my life."
12.	—	—	—	"I ask for support from adults I'm close to when I need it."

Checkmarks for Questions 1–4 may indicate some dismissive tendencies. Checkmarks for Questions 5–8 may indicate some preoccupied tendencies. A checkmark for Question 9 may indicate an unresolved/disorganized tendency. Checkmarks for Questions

10–12 indicate security. You may identify with more than one attachment pattern. And remember, the labels are not the goal. It's about recognizing which tendencies are working and which are not working in your close relationships.

If you identify with dismissive, preoccupied, or disorganized attachment patterns, it's important for you to know that your patterns in relationships can shift toward increased security through new, positive relationship experiences or mental health therapy. In a case study of three adults with insecure or disorganized patterns, EMDR therapy facilitated a shift toward greater attachment security for each individual (Wesselmann & Potter, 2009).

SETTLING THE CHILD PART OF YOU ON THE INSIDE

Your child's difficult behaviors, such as defiance, stealing, and lying may trigger vulnerable feelings that take you back to feelings associated with difficult times when you were a kid. When triggered, those old feelings may activate a hurt child part of you and move you into a fight-or-flight or shutdown zone where you lose access to your skills for attunement and connection.

When we find ourselves struggling with triggers, a fired-up nervous system, and feelings carried forward from our own childhood, it helps to consciously anchor ourselves in our most grounded, competent adult state. What body posture is associated with your most competent adult state? Does it help to plant your feet on the floor and stand or sit up with your shoulders down and back? Does it help to keep your head up and your arms by your sides?

Find your competent adult body posture. Place a hand over your heart and think of the child part of you enfolded with a warm, healing light, tucked safely inside of you. Remind that child part of you that the present is now and the past is over. Try doing this any time you're struggling emotionally.

PARTICIPATING IN YOUR OWN THERAPY

If you're struggling with feelings associated with the child part of you, a therapist can help you heal the old feelings and experiences. Many parents of traumatized children involved in therapy have found engaging in their own therapy to be invaluable. Your child's therapist may be able to help you find a therapist who's a good match for you.

An EMDR therapist can help you reach stored, "stuck" trauma, emotions, and beliefs, reduce intense emotions, and make new meaning of the events in your life. EMDR can help remove the power from those earlier events and their impact on your thoughts and feelings today. Whether you choose to work with an EMDR therapist, engage in another type of therapy, or participate in a therapy group, you will move toward finding satisfaction as a parent and in your life overall.

- *List positive affirmations that would be helpful for you.* Type the affirmations into your phone so you can read them daily. (Here's a few statements to get you started. These statements are universally true: "I don't have to be perfect with anything at all," "I'm worthy and good as I am," "I can grow through all of my experiences," "I can give myself grace.")

  _____

  _____

  _____

  _____

- *Make plans for self-care.* (Here's a few ideas to get you started: A lunch date with a friend. Joining or forming a book club. Attending counseling. Joining a parent organization or group. Daily meditation. Yoga or some other form of exercise. Reaching out for help with childcare. Engaging or reengaging in a hobby. Letting go of unnecessary commitments.)

  _____

  _____

_____

_____

• *List any habits/attitudes you'd like to change.*

_____

_____

_____

_____

• *List changes you want to make as a parent.*

_____

_____

_____

_____

Helping your child heal from attachment trauma may be one of the hardest challenges you've ever faced—perhaps the hardest. But few things matter more than giving a child the gift of a new trajectory. So summon all the self-compassion and self-care you can to stay the course. You don't have to do it alone—reach out and gather the support you need.

Closing Thoughts

I SUPPOSE IT WOULD BE SIMPLER if we could make our kids be good people by just punishing them for misbehavior and rewarding them for good behavior. But it doesn't work that way—and it never will.

When our kids have learned that we truly love them and see them and hear them, they begin looking up to us. Only then do we have the power to *inspire* them to *grow into* the good people they were always meant to be.

References

Ainsworth, M. D. S. (1982). Attachment: Retrospect and prospect. In C. M. Parkes & J. Stevenson-Hinde (Eds.), *The place of attachment in human behavior* (pp. 3–29). Tavistock.

American Psychiatric Association. (2013). *Diagnostic and statistical manual of mental disorders* (5th ed.).

Boss, P. (2000). *Ambiguous loss: Learning to live with unresolved grief.* Harvard University Press.

BRAIN-Online (2023). FASD United. Available at www.fasdunited.org/brain-online/

California Evidence-Based Clearinghouse for Child Welfare. (2010). Available at www.cebc4cw.org/program/eye-movement-desensitization-and-reprocessing

Chasnoff, I. J., Wells, A. M., & King, L. (2015). Misdiagnosis and missed diagnosis in foster and adopted children with prenatal alcohol exposure. *Pediatrics, 135*(2), 264–270.

Cline, F., & Fay, J. (2006). *Parenting teens with love and logic: Preparing adolescents for responsible adulthood.* NavPress.

Dreckmeier-Meiring, M. (2024, April). Integrative eye movement desensitization and reprocessing and family therapy model for treating attachment trauma: Possibilities in the New Zealand context. *Journal of the New Zealand College of Clinical Psychologists, 34*(1), 4–13. doi:10.5281/zenodo.10939122

Fadeeva, E., & Nenasteva, A. (2022). Diagnostic results of IQ-test in school-aged children with fetal alcohol syndrome and fetal alcohol spectrum of disorders. *European Psychiatry, 65*(Suppl. 1), S421.

Farkas, B. F., Takacs, Z. K., Kollarovics, N., & Balazs, J. (2024). The prevalence of self-injury in adolescence: A systematic review and meta-analysis. *European Child and Adolescent Psychiatry, 33,* 3439–3458.

Fonagy, P., Target, M., Steele, M., Steele, H., Leigh, T., Levinson, A., & Kennedy, R. (1997). Morality, disruptive behavior, borderline personality disorder, crime, and their relationships to security of attachment. In L. Atkinson & K. J. Zucker (Eds.), *Attachment and psychopathology* (pp. 223–274). Guilford Press.

Greene, R. (2021). *The explosive child: A new approach for understanding and parenting easily frustrated, chronically inflexible children.* Harper.

Hesse, E. (1999). The Adult Attachment Interview: Historical and current perspectives.

In J. Cassidy & P. R. Shaver (Eds.), *Handbook of attachment: Theory, research, and clinical applications* (pp. 395–433). Guilford Press.

Levine, P. A. (2010). *In an unspoken voice: How the body releases trauma and restores goodness*. North Atlantic Books.

Malbin, D. (2017). *Trying differently rather than harder* (2nd ed.). FASCETS.

Mattson, S. N., Jones, K. L., Chockalingam, G., Wozniak, J. R., Hyland, M. T., Courchesne-Krak, N. S., Del Campo, M., Riley, E. P., & CIFASD. (2023). Validation of the FASD-Tree as a screening tool for fetal alcohol spectrum disorders. *Alcohol, Clinical and Experimental Research, 47*(2), 263–272. https://doi.org/10.1111/acer.14987

Molock, S. D., Boyd, R. C., Alvarez, K., Cha, C., Denton, E., Glenn, C. R., Katz, C. C., Mueller, A. S., Meca, A., Meza, J. I., Miranda, R., Ortin-Peralta, A., Polanco-Roman, L., Singer, J. B., Zullo, L., & Miller, A. B. (2023). Culturally responsive assessment of suicidal thoughts and behaviors in youth of color. *American Psychologist, 78*, 842–355.

National Institute for Health and Care Excellence. (2018). *Guidelines for posttraumatic stress disorder*.

National Resources Directory (2023). University of Washington Fetal Alcohol and Drug Unit. www.fadu.psychiatry.uw.edu/resources

Ogden, P., Minton, K., & Pain, C. (2006). *Trauma and the body: A sensorimotor approach to psychotherapy*. Norton.

Porges, S. W. (2009). The polyvagal theory: New insights into adaptive reactions of the autonomic nervous system. *Cleveland Clinic Journal of Medicine, 76*(Suppl. 2), 86–90. doi:10.3949/ccjm.76.s2.17

Potter, A. E. (2011a). *The anatomy of a meltdown* [Unpublished manuscript].

Potter, A. E. (2011b). *The domino effect* [Unpublished manuscript].

Purvis, K. B., Cross, D. R., & Sunshine, W. L. (2007). *The connected child: Bring hope and healing to your adopted family*. McGraw-Hill.

Shapiro, F. (2018). *Eye movement desensitization and reprocessing: Basic principles, protocols, and procedures* (3rd ed.). Guilford Press.

Siegel, D. J. (1999). *The developing mind: Toward a neurobiology of interpersonal experience*. Guilford Press.

Siegel, D. J., & Bryson, T. P. (2011). *The wholebrain child: 12 revolutionary strategies to nurture your child's developing mind*. Bantam Books.

Swimm, L. L. (2018). EMDR intervention for a 17-month-old child to treat attachment trauma: Clinical case presentation. *Journal of EMDR Practice and Research, 12*, 269–281.

Teicher, M. H., Samson, J. A., Anderson C. M., & Ohashi, K. (2016). The effects of childhood maltreatment on brain structure, function and connectivity. *Nature Reviews. Neuroscience, 12*(10), 652–666.

van der Hoeven, M. L., Plukaard, S. C., Schlattmann, N. E. F., Lindauer, R. J. L., & Hein, I. M. (2023). An integrative treatment model of EMDR and family therapy for children after child abuse and neglect: A SCED study. *Children and Youth Services Review, 152*, 1–12.

van der Kolk, B. A. (2005). Developmental trauma disorder: Toward a rational diagnosis for children with complex trauma histories. *Psychiatric Annals, 35*(5), 401–408.

Wesselmann, D. (2025). *EMDR and family therapy: Integrative treatment for attachment trauma in children.* Norton.

Wesselmann, D., Armstrong, S., Schweitzer, C., Davidson, M., & Potter, A. (2018). An integrative EMDR and family therapy model for treating attachment trauma in children: A case series. *Journal of EMDR Practice and Research, 12*, 196–207.

Wesselmann, D., & Potter, A. E. (2009). Change in adult attachment status following treatment with EMDR: Three case studies. *Journal of EMDR Practice and Research, 3*(3), 178–191.

Wollin, E. L. (2023, September). *The impact of prenatal substance exposure to substances on children.* Presentation sponsored by Mother's Choice and Adoptive Families of Hong Kong.

World Health Organization. (2013). *Guidelines for the management of conditions that are specifically related to stress.*

Index

Note: Italicized page locators refer to figures.

Index

About the Author

Debra Wesselmann, MS, LIMHP, has been dedicated to helping children, adults, and families heal from the effects of attachment trauma for over thirty years. Through her clinical work and research, she was instrumental in developing an integrative family and EMDR therapy model specifically for treating attachment trauma in children. Debra has authored and coauthored numerous books, articles, and book chapters, and teaches for the EMDR Institute, founded by Francine Shapiro, PhD, where she also helped create a child-focused training. A sought-after speaker, Debra presents keynotes and workshops across the U.S. and internationally.